Individuals & Societies

MYP by Concept

2

Paul Grace

Series editor: Paul Morris

Author's acknowledgements

This book is dedicated to my friends and family.

I'd like to thank So-Shan Au, Megan Price, Emilie Kerton, Estelle Lloyd and Paul Morris for all their help and support with this project.

Although every effort has been made to ensure that website addresses are correct at time of going to press, Hodder Education cannot be held responsible for the content of any website mentioned in this book. It is sometimes possible to find a relocated web page by typing in the address of the home page for a website in the URL window of your browser.

Hachette UK's policy is to use papers that are natural, renewable and recyclable products and made from wood grown in well-managed forests and other controlled sources. The logging and manufacturing processes are expected to conform to the environmental regulations of the country of origin.

Orders: please contact Hachette UK Distribution, Hely Hutchinson Centre, Milton Road, Didcot, Oxfordshire, OX11 7HH. Telephone: +44 (0)1235 827827. Email **education@hachette.co.uk**
Lines are open from 9 a.m. to 5 p.m., Monday to Friday. You can also order through our website **www.hoddereducation.com**.

© Paul Grace 2016
Published by Hodder Education (a trading division of Hodder & Stoughton Limited),
An Hachette UK Company
Carmelite House
50 Victoria Embankment
London EC4Y 0DZ

The authorised representative in the EEA is Hachette Ireland, 8 Castlecourt Centre, Dublin 15, D15 XTP3, Ireland (email: info@hbgi.ie)

Impression number   15

Year   2025

All rights reserved. Apart from any use permitted under UK copyright law, no part of this publication may be reproduced or transmitted in any form or by any means, electronic or mechanical, including photocopying and recording, or held within any information storage and retrieval system, without permission in writing from the publisher or under licence from the Copyright Licensing Agency Limited. Further details of such licences (for reprographic reproduction) may be obtained from the Copyright Licensing Agency Limited, www.cla.co.uk

Cover photo © Rawpixel Ltd/Thinkstock/iStockphoto/Getty Images
Illustrations by DC Graphic Design Limited and Jim Eldridge/Oxford Designers & Illustrators
Typeset in Frutiger LT Std 45 Light 11/15pt by DC Graphic Design Limited, Hextable, Kent
Printed and bound in Great Britain by Bell and Bain Ltd, Glasgow

A catalogue record for this title is available from the British Library

ISBN: 9781471880261

Contents

1. How has globalization shaped the world? 2
2. Why are natural environments important to individuals and societies? 24
3. What was life like in the Middle Ages? 54
4. How does exploration affect global interactions? 80
5. How can energy be produced sustainably? 108
6. How have innovations and ideas changed the world? 128

Glossary 150

Acknowledgements 152

Index 154

How to use this book

Welcome to Hodder Education's *MYP by Concept* series! Each chapter is designed to lead you through an inquiry into the concepts of Individuals and societies, and how they interact in real-life global contexts.

Each chapter is framed with a *Key concept* and a *Related concept* and is set in a *Global context*.

The *Statement of Inquiry* provides the framework for this inquiry, and the *Inquiry questions* then lead us through the exploration as they are developed through each chapter.

KEY WORDS

Key words are included to give you access to vocabulary for the topic. **Glossary** terms are highlighted and, where applicable, **search terms** are given to encourage independent learning and research skills.

As you explore, activities suggest ways to learn through *action*.

■ ATL

Activities are designed to develop your *Approaches to Learning* (ATL) skills.

EXTENSION

Extension activities allow you to explore a topic further.

◆ Assessment opportunities in this chapter:

Some activities are *formative* as they allow you to practise certain parts of the MYP Individuals and societies *Assessment Objectives*. Other activities can be used by you or your teachers to assess your achievement against all parts of an assessment objective.

Key *Approaches to Learning* skills for MYP Individuals and societies are highlighted whenever we encounter them.

Hint

In some of the activities, we provide hints to help you work on the assignment. This also introduces you to the new Hint feature in the on-screen assessment.

 Information boxes are included to give more detail and explanation.

You are prompted to consider your conceptual understanding in a variety of activities throughout each chapter.

We have incorporated Visible Thinking – ideas, framework, protocol and thinking routines – from Project Zero at the Harvard Graduate School of Education into many of our activities.

Finally, at the end of the chapter you are asked to reflect back on what you have learned with our *Reflection table*, maybe to think of new questions brought to light by your learning.

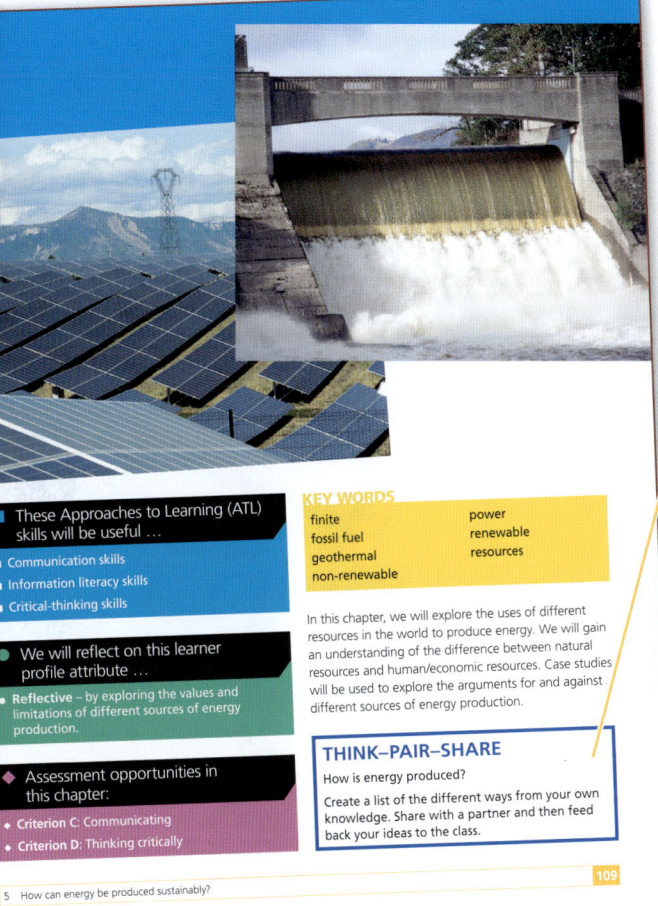

Use this table to reflect on your own learning in this chapter.						
Questions we asked	Answers we found	Any further questions now?				
Factual						
Conceptual						
Debatable						
Approaches to learning you used in this chapter:	Description – what new skills did you learn?	How well did you master the skills?				
		Novice	Learner	Practitioner	Expert	
Learner profile attribute(s)	Reflect on the importance of the attribute for your learning in this chapter.					

! Take action

! While the book provides *opportunities* for action and plenty of content to enrich the conceptual relationships, you must be an active part of this process. Guidance is given to help you with your own research, including how to carry out research, guidance on forming your own research question, as well as linking and developing your study of individuals and societies to the global issues in our twenty-first-century world.

▼ Links to:

Like any other subject, individuals and societies is just one part of our bigger picture of the world. Links to other subjects are discussed.

● We will reflect on this learner profile attribute …

Each chapter has an *IB learner profile* attribute as its theme, and you are encouraged to reflect on these too.

Change　　　　Globalization; Processes　　　　Globalization and sustainability

1 How has globalization shaped the world?

○ **Globalization** has occurred due to a variety of **processes** that have **changed the world**, bringing both **opportunities and challenges**.

CONSIDER THESE QUESTIONS:

Factual: What is globalization? What are transnational corporations? How has globalization affected sport? How has globalization affected the gaming industry?

Conceptual: What are the causes of globalization? How has globalization affected language?

Debatable: Is globalization new? Is there such a thing as a global culture?

Now **share and compare** your thoughts and ideas with your partner, or with the whole class.

■ **Figure 1.1** Globalization in business and the classroom

┌─ IN THIS CHAPTER, WE WILL …
■ **Find out** about the causes and consequences of globalization.
■ **Explore** examples of globalization in language, business, sport and entertainment.
■ **Take action** by looking at the ways that globalization can promote positive change.

■ **Figure 1.2** A map of the world

■ These Approaches to Learning (ATL) skills will be useful …
- Communication skills
- Reflection skills
- Information literacy skills
- Critical-thinking skills
- Creative-thinking skills

● We will reflect on this learner profile attribute …
- Caring – by making connections to global issues that result from the process of globalization.

◆ Assessment opportunities in this chapter:
- Criterion A: Knowing and understanding
- Criterion C: Communicating
- Criterion D: Thinking critically

ACTIVITY: The world at a glance

- How many countries can you **identify** on this map of the world?
- How many continents can you name?
- Are there any areas of the world that you have no idea about?

Use an atlas to check your understanding.

You can test your knowledge of world geography further with the 'Traveller IQ Challenge' from www.travelpod.com.

KEY WORDS
companies
corporations
industry

1 How has globalization shaped the world?

What is globalization?

Have you ever heard people say that the world is getting smaller? Sometimes it seems that the world is becoming so interconnected that the large distances between places are becoming less important. We can have video calls with people on the other side of the world, work collaboratively with people in different continents and travel to practically anywhere.

The process that has allowed this to occur is called **globalization**. Developments in transport, communications and trade have all helped this process to take place. Nowadays it feels that the speed of globalization is increasing more rapidly as the internet has an ever-increasing influence over our daily lives, meaning that we can connect with people all over the world.

> ## DISCUSS
> Take a look at Source A, which shows the proportion of people using the internet in different areas of the world. **Discuss** these questions:
> 1 What is the significance of having access to the internet?
> 2 How would lack of internet access restrict people's lives?

SOURCE A

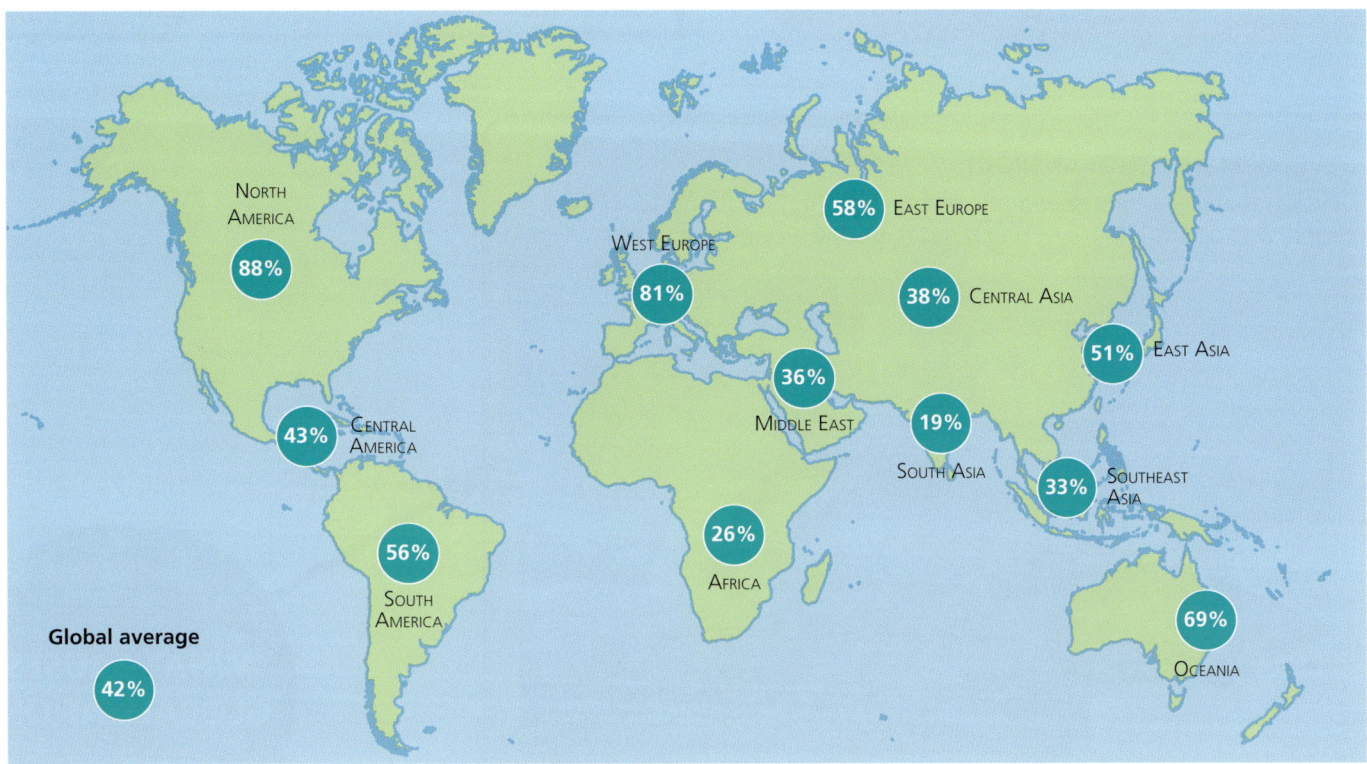

■ **Figure 1.3** Global internet usage, January 2015

What are the causes of globalization?

> **DISCUSS**
> Take a look at the mind map on the causes of globalization. **Discuss** the different ways that each of the causes might affect the world.

DEVELOPMENTS IN TRANSPORT:
Developments like high-speed rail, cargo shipping and flight mean that people and goods can travel much more quickly around the world.

WHAT CAUSES GLOBALIZATION?

COMMUNICATIONS:
The increased speed and versatility of internet technology has allowed for far greater and effective connectivity between people across the globe. In addition, the use of mobile technology and wearable technology is ever-increasing this process and affecting our working and social lives.

■ **Figure 1.4** The causes of globalization

TRADE:
Many countries have trading agreements that allow for the exchange of goods with relative ease. The World Trade Organization (WTO) is an international organization that plays an important role in improving global trade conditions.

LABOUR AVAILABILITY:
Workers are no longer confined to their geographic location for work – this is due to **migration**. Migrant workers travel to different countries to work in different capacities. This can bring economic benefits to the workers but can also present challenges in terms of working conditions. Workers in economically developing countries can be used by international companies to reduce costs. Building a factory in an economically developing country can be significantly more economically beneficial in terms of profits.

1   How has globalization shaped the world?

Is globalization new?

We can argue that the world has become more interconnected throughout the last centuries. Take a look at the following inventions. How do you think they would have affected the world?

- The wheel during ancient times
- The printing press during the Renaissance
- The steam train during the 19th century
- Commercial flights during the 20th century
- The internet in the 21st century

■ **Figure 1.5** The wheel and the printing press. How do you think these inventions affected the world?

You could say that globalization isn't actually new. For example, imagine you were living in a town that had just had a railway station built during the 19th century. You can now travel far more easily to locations that in the past may have taken you several days to get to. Or imagine the differences in travelling around the world in the era before commercial flights were a common feature of life.

The counter argument, however, is that the speed of globalization has been rapidly increasing in the last few decades and especially in the 21st century. This is due to many of the communications breakthroughs that have greatly affected the world. In this chapter, we will explore different examples of globalization and focus on the opportunities and challenges each example presents for the world.

> **REFLECTION**
>
> Make two mind maps: one called 'What is globalization?'; the second 'Is globalization new?' **Use** some of the ideas from here and add in your own thoughts to reflect on these introductory questions to the chapter.

How has globalization affected language?

An interesting area where we can see the consequences of globalization is that of language. Over the last century, English has in many ways and for many reasons become the preferred language of globalization, even though there are more speakers of Mandarin Chinese worldwide.

We can see that globally a small number of languages dominate international business and commerce. These tend to be English, Spanish, Mandarin Chinese and Arabic. One of the side effects of this development is the marginalization of languages spoken by smaller numbers of people. Many linguists are concerned about languages that are on the verge of extinction due to this development. However, cultural and national identity protects these languages as many people seek to maintain their traditions by speaking their mother tongue language.

One interesting example of the mixing of languages is that of 'Chinglish'. This is a slang term for when the Chinese language is translated into English but continues to contain aspects of both languages and becomes ungrammatical or nonsensical English in a Chinese context.

The widespread use of English also means that new words are created that reflect cultural and social developments at the time. For instance, the term 'selfie' is an example of a word that has emerged as a result of the global technological developments of mobile phones.

> **REFLECTION**
>
> **List** what you think are the positive and negative consequences of the increased use of English globally.

▼ Links to: Language and literature

Examples of 'new' words added to the English language:

athleisure (n): casual clothing designed to be worn both for exercising and for general use

hella (adv, slang): very, extremely

nomophobia (n): fear of being without access to a working cell phone

By permission. From Merriam-Webster's Collegiate® Dictionary, 11th Edition © 2016 by Merriam-Webster, Inc. (www.Merriam-Webster.com)

Discuss with a partner any other new words you can think of that have come into common usage in recent years. What do the words teach us about global culture?

> **REFLECTION**
>
> In pairs, **discuss** this question: Are there certain shared values and practices that people have all over the world?

SOURCE A

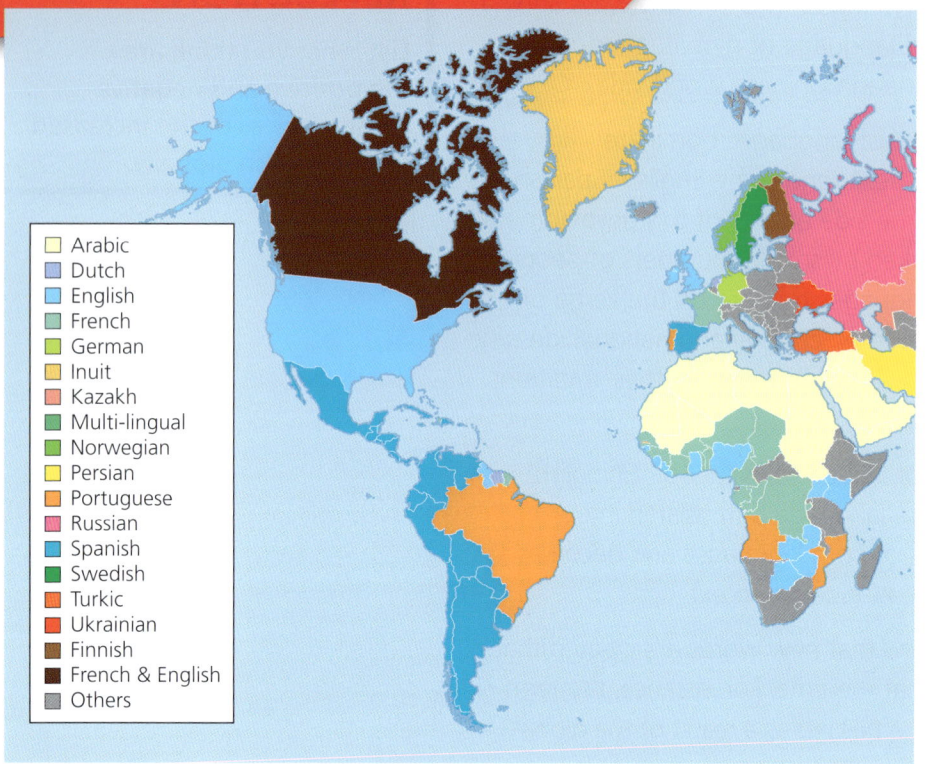

Copyright © www.mapsofworld.com

■ **Figure 1.6** Languages spoken around parts of the world

SOURCE B

■ **Figure 1.7** An example of Chinglish

SOURCE C

Extract about some languages disappearing and how this could be prevented

It is estimated that, if nothing is done, half of 6,000 plus languages spoken today will disappear by the end of this century. With the disappearance of unwritten and undocumented languages, humanity would lose not only a cultural wealth but also important ancestral knowledge embedded, in particular, in indigenous languages.

However, this process is neither inevitable nor irreversible: well-planned and implemented language policies can bolster the ongoing efforts of speaker communities to maintain or revitalize their mother tongues and pass them on to younger generations.

SOURCE D

Extract about the number of languages threatened in the world

After crunching the numbers using data culled from the Ethnologue, an authoritative source for basic information about the world's languages, the researchers concluded that 25 percent of the world's languages are in immediate danger of disappearing forever.

SOURCE E

Extract about how technology can help preserve threatened languages

There is now cause for hope. While the dispersal of speech communities across the globe has led to the demise of some languages, technology popularized by globalization is playing an equally important role in their revitalization. Through the internet and mobile communications, people are reconnecting with fellow speakers using digital tools to revive languages on the endangered list …

Many speakers of endangered, poorly documented languages have embraced new digital media with excitement. Speakers of previously exclusively oral tongues are turning to the web as a virtual space for languages to live on. Internet technology offers powerful ways for oral traditions and cultural practices to survive, even thrive, among increasingly mobile communities.

SOURCE F

■ **Figure 1.8** Speakers of the language Euchee, a threatened Native American language. The two sisters visit the grave of their grandfather in Oklahoma, USA

ACTIVITY: Globalization and language

■ ATL

Information literacy skills – Make connections between various sources of information

1. Study Source A. Write down three things that the map tells you about the spread of languages spoken around the world.
2. What do you understand by the term 'Chinglish'? Why do you think languages merge together? Can you think of other examples?
3. What do Sources C, D and E suggest about the threats facing languages in the world?
4. What does Source E suggest about the ways that endangered languages can be protected? **List** any other ways you can think of.

◆ Assessment opportunities

This activity can be assessed using Criterion D: Thinking critically (strands i, ii and iv).

1 How has globalization shaped the world?

What are transnational corporations?

Globalization has seen the creation of very large companies or corporations that exist in multiple countries. This process began in the era of **industrialization**, during which companies were able to mass-produce goods and then ship them around the world. For example, the globalization of the car industry in the 20th century has meant that there are Japanese cars in Europe and German cars in China.

In the last few decades of the 20th century this process led to the development of **transnational corporations (TNCs)** that exist in multiple countries. For example, companies like Starbucks Coffee and McDonald's can be seen in countries all over the world.

Transnational corporations are companies that exist in more than one country.

Often, transnational corporations are able to spread around the world due to the creation of **franchises**. Franchises are permissions from a company or government to set up a commercial venture in a particular location. So, even though Starbucks originally started in Seattle, USA, there are franchises (i.e. replica businesses) all over the world that sell the same products. Profits are kept within the Starbucks brand but individuals are able to create their own profits through the managing and running of the individual branches.

■ **Figure 1.9** A global brand

> **DISCUSS**
>
> What do you think are examples of global brands? In pairs, **list** as many as you can think of.

Another feature of transnational corporations is their methods of production. Production refers to the creation of the different goods for sale. For example, shoe companies need to create their products somewhere and turn out a quality product every time. This has often led to the production of goods in locations where relatively cheap labour can be used while also ensuring the quality of production. Many products in the world have a 'Made in China' tag on them due to the huge extent of manufacturing that has occurred in the country since the 1980s.

It is not just China, however, that has been at the forefront of manufacturing for transnational corporations. Other locations such as Indonesia, Brazil and Taiwan have increased their output in recent years. There has also been a tendency for companies to use labour and factories in **developing countries** in order to reduce costs.

■ **Figure 1.10** Factory workers

POSITIVE	NEGATIVE
• Choice and consistency of quality of products delivered by TNCs	• Can serve the interests of economically developed countries over economically developing countries
• Global brands mean that people can access TNC products around the world	• Can potentially exploit cheaper workers with long working hours and difficult conditions
• Investment in countries, for example creation of jobs in countries where manufacturing is set up	• Can lead to a reduction in manufacturing in more economically developed countries as companies prefer to go with cheaper options in less economically developed countries
• Can help to develop workforce skills for particular goods and services	• Can have a negative environmental impact due to emissions and waste produced by different factories
• TNCs can serve for good, for instance promoting sustainability and environmental issues	

■ **Table 1.1** What are the positive and negative consequences of transnational corporations?

Development terminology and politics

You will have seen that on page 13, the last sentence talks about companies using labour and factories in developing countries in order to reduce costs. Which countries do they outsource the work to? Is China a developing or **developed country**?

Find out what countries are categorised **developing countries** and **developed countries**. What other terms could be used to categorize countries?

Economists like to use:
- Low-income countries (LIC)
- Medium-income countries (MIC)
- High-income countries (HIC)

Search for the following: **LEDC, MEDC, LEC, LIC HIC, MIC** and discuss the differences with a partner. Why are LEDC and MEDC no longer used?

■ **Figure 1.11** What factors would a clothing manufacturer need to consider when deciding where to set up a new factory?

EXTENSION

Find out more about **ethical fashion**, **fast fashion** and search the hashtag **#whomademyclothes** to learn more about the fashion industry's attempts to be more ethical.

ACTIVITY: Decision-making

ATL

- Reflection skills – Consider ethical, cultural and environmental implications
- Critical-thinking skills – Recognize and evaluate propositions

A TNC from France that manufactures clothes and sells them in its shops around the world is looking for a new location to create its products. In the past it has done all of its manufacturing in China but costs have been increasing. The company is keen to save money but wants to promote ethical practices in terms of the working conditions for the people in the factory. It has been given the following options:

- **Option 1**: Country A. Costs: relatively high; working conditions: excellent
- **Option 2**: Country B. Costs: relatively cheap; working conditions: good
- **Option 3**: Country C. Costs: very cheap; working conditions: average

Consider the following perspectives:

- **CEO of the company in France:** Very keen to save money but also concerned about the image of the company. Would like to ensure that people are treated fairly in the factory
- **Consumer:** Loves the clothes that the TNC creates and is a regular shopper, but conscious of the importance of good working conditions for the people who produce the clothes
- **Factory owner in Country A:** Workers' salaries are quite high and there are many laws protecting workers' rights
- **Factory worker in Country C:** Work is quite hard in the factory and salaries are quite low but on the whole conditions are improving
- **Factory worker in Country B:** Working hours are long but there is the option to work extra hours or not. Conditions are generally good but wages could be better considering the hard work

In groups of three, each person should write up a short proposal for one of the options. **Explain** why you would like to work with this country. **Discuss** each proposal. Finally, decide as a group which option you think is the best.

◆ Assessment opportunities

In this activity you have practised skills that are assessed using Criterion D: Thinking critically (strands ii and iv).

How has globalization affected sport?

■ **Figure 1.12** Cristiano Ronaldo is a global sports celebrity

Global sport is a major commercial industry. In recent years, a number of sports have massively increased their global popularity. Sports such as football, baseball and basketball are played all over the world and watched by people via new technologies that bring the games into the home. The men's World Cup Final in 2014 received 32 million tweets on the social media site Twitter during the game (see Figure 1.13). People can connect with others during a sports game to share their opinions and ideas on how it is going.

The spread of sports around the world is staggering – we can see how international sports have become by observing the top players in the world. Top basketball players are now not just from the USA and top football players are not just from Europe or Latin America.

Transnational corporations play a huge role within the sports industry, from being the company that airs the game to being the corporate sponsor. Huge amounts of money are spent on the presentation and showing of games, including money from advertising and buying the rights to air the game. Some sports figures are paid huge sums of money to wear a particular brand and salaries for the elite players are very high.

SOURCE A

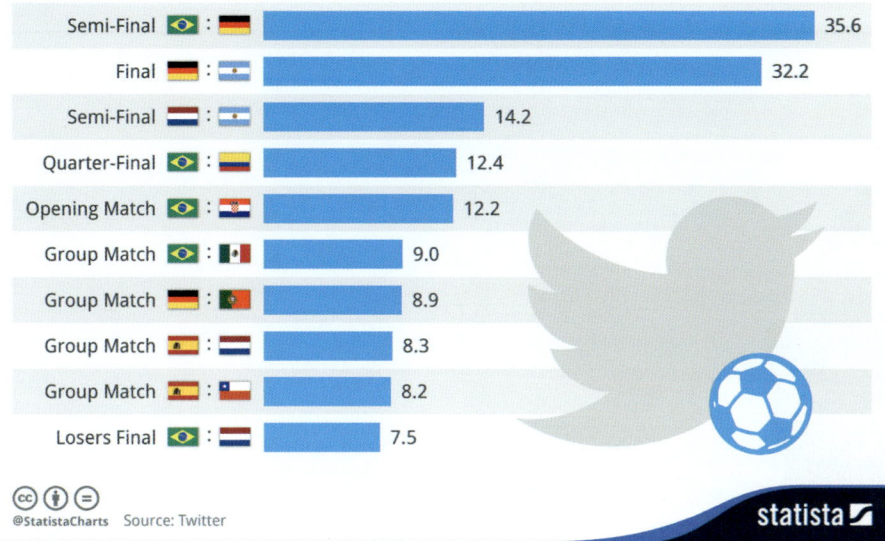

■ **Figure 1.13** FIFA World Cup, 2014

SOURCE B

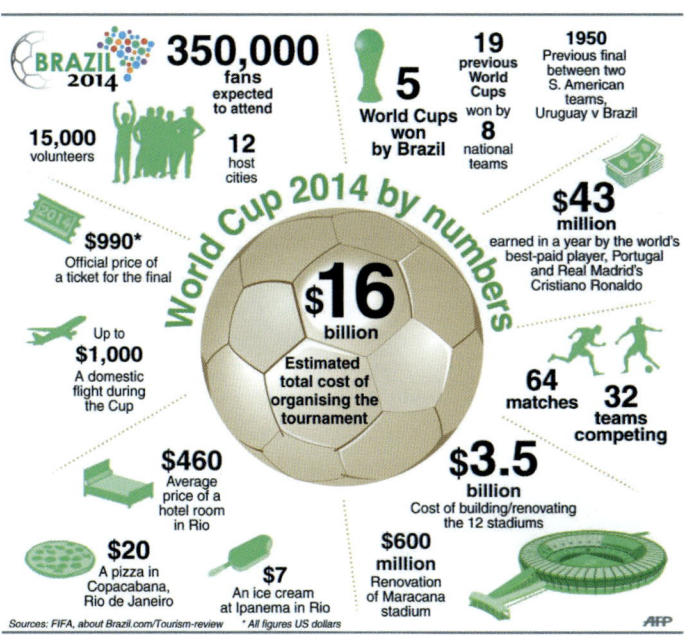

■ **Figure 1.14** World Cup 2014 statistics

1 How has globalization shaped the world?

SOURCE C

By Forest Whitaker 2016

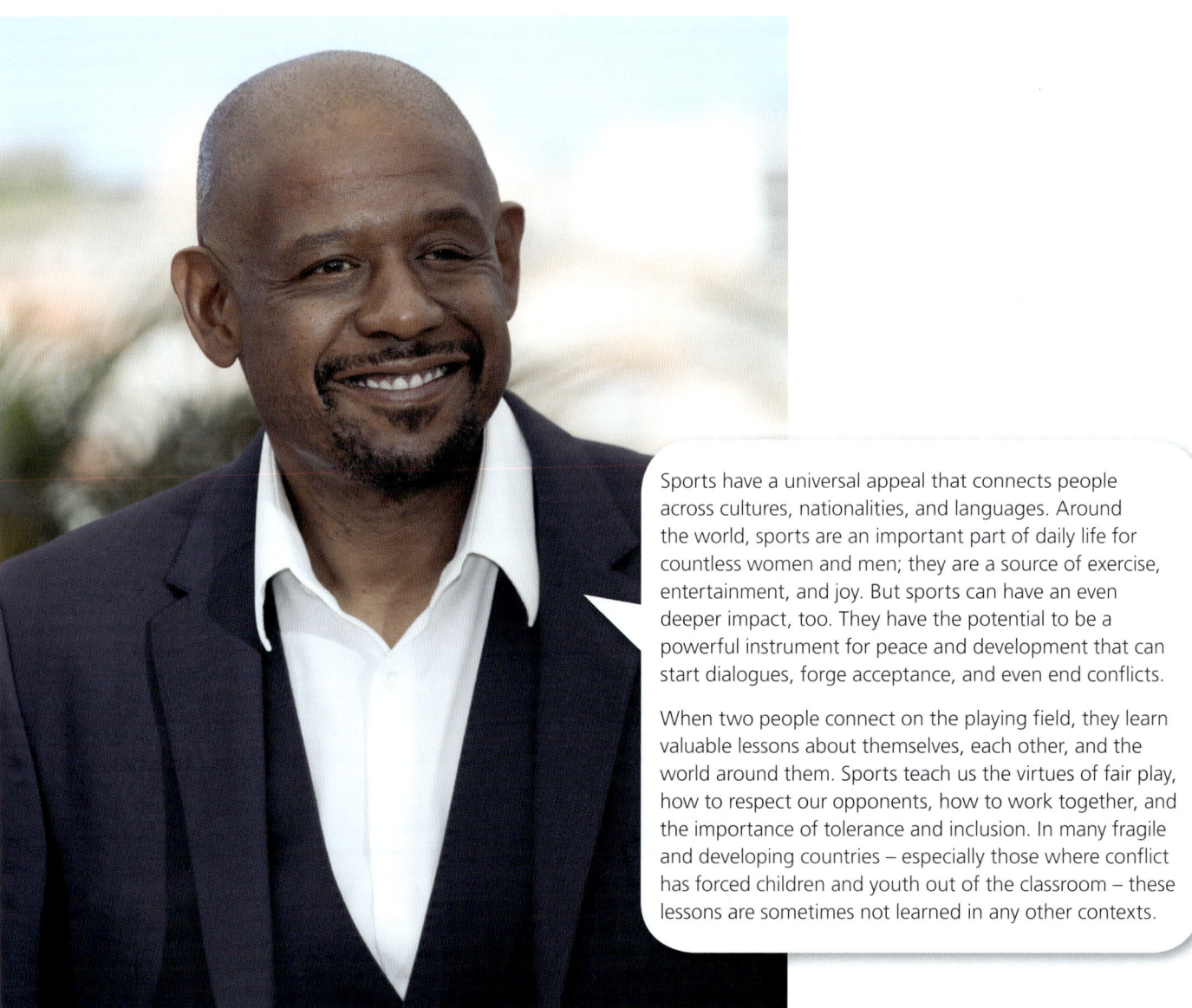

Sports have a universal appeal that connects people across cultures, nationalities, and languages. Around the world, sports are an important part of daily life for countless women and men; they are a source of exercise, entertainment, and joy. But sports can have an even deeper impact, too. They have the potential to be a powerful instrument for peace and development that can start dialogues, forge acceptance, and even end conflicts.

When two people connect on the playing field, they learn valuable lessons about themselves, each other, and the world around them. Sports teach us the virtues of fair play, how to respect our opponents, how to work together, and the importance of tolerance and inclusion. In many fragile and developing countries – especially those where conflict has forced children and youth out of the classroom – these lessons are sometimes not learned in any other contexts.

■ **Figure 1.15** Oscar-winning actor, peace activist and UNESCO Goodwill Ambassador for Peace and Reconciliation, Forest Whitaker

www.wpdi.org/blog/promoting-peace-and-development-and-playing-field

ACTIVITY: World Cup in numbers

■ ATL

Communication skills – Write for different purposes

1 What does Source A suggest about the role of social media (for example Twitter, Facebook) during major sports competitions? Do you think that this has any commercial value?
2 What does Source B suggest about the different ways that major sporting events have an economic effect? Who do you think stands to benefit from these different examples?
3 Study Source C. What points does Forest Whitaker make about how sport can have a positive impact on the world?
4 Choose a recent sporting event, such as the Olympics or World Cup, and create an infographic to represent the event. Go online to find data. The website www.statista.com may be of use here.

◆ Assessment opportunities

In this activity you have practised skills that are assessed using Criterion C: Communicating (strands i, ii and iii).

▼ Links to: Mathematics

What do you think are the values and limitations of using statistics to understand major sporting competitions?

Designing infographics

Infographics display data in a creative way. They are really useful as a form of communication. A good idea when creating an infographic is to spend a bit of time researching your topic and finding a good range of relevant statistics. Then try to think of creative ways that you can present the data, for example you could create images that are relevant to the specific statistic. Try to have an overall theme and be aware of your use of colour.

How has globalization affected the gaming industry?

Large numbers of people around the world have been affected by the developments surrounding the internet. Connectivity, speed and the user experience have improved in recent years. The gaming industry has changed considerably as a result of these developments.

Computer games have been around for a long time, with people playing them throughout the 1980s and 1990s. Old consoles from Nintendo and Sega now seem like antiques in comparison to recent models (see Figure 1.16).

Gamers no longer need to play in isolation and can now compete or collaborate with other players around the world. In many countries, for example Japan and South Korea, online gaming is so popular that the top gamers are often treated as celebrities. The online interface allows people to create social networks where people game together. This means that people can build strong friendships with fellow gamers in other parts of the world. The different games can also lead to the development of skills such as hand–eye coordination, reaction time and problem solving. If used well, they also encourage healthy competition.

However, there are critics of these developments in gaming. One fear is the rise of gaming addiction, as large amounts of time can be spent playing online games which may reduce time spent talking with people in the home or school, playing sports or generally interacting off the computer. Another concern is the level of violence in specific games.

Whatever your opinion, there is no doubting the vast impact of online gaming on the entertainments industry which will only continue to grow in the future.

■ **Figure 1.16** The speed of technological changes has had a big impact on the computer games industry as models change relatively frequently over the years

SOURCE A

■ **Figure 1.17** Pro-gamers in South Korea

SOURCE B

South Korea considers creating a bill to combat online gaming

South Korea's parliament is considering an anti-gaming bill that will classify online gaming as a potentially antisocial addiction alongside gambling, drugs and alcohol.

The bill is backed by 14 ruling party lawmakers, parents, religious groups and doctors who believe that online gaming is having a negative effect on schooling, family life and work.

'Without online games, kids would talk to their mother and play,' said Kim Min-sun, a mother of two who supports the bill …

If passed, the law will put a limit on gaming advertising and build a fund to fight gaming addiction by ordering the gaming industry to hand over one percent of their revenue.

http://thediplomat.com/2013/12/south-korea-considers-bill-to-combat-online-gaming/

SOURCE C

In the United States alone, an estimated 99 percent of boys and 94 percent of girls play video games with 97 percent playing at least one hour per day. The revenue from the video game industry topped $25 billion dollars in 2010 alone and video games have become an important part of popular culture …

Although there is no question that ordinary play can provide a wide range of benefits for young people, does the sort of play allowed by interactive video games produce the same benefits? … Isabela Granic and her co-researchers argue that it does. Not only do video games allow players to interact with the game systems in a way that would not be possible for more passive forms of entertainment such as movies or television, but they can be played either alone, with others, or in competition with thousands of other online players.

www.psychologytoday.com/blog/media-spotlight/201402/are-there-benefits-in-playing-video-games

---

THINK–PAIR–SHARE

Think about some of the arguments for and against online gaming. Look at Sources A–C and **discuss** with a partner. Did you come up with the same points?

Share your thoughts with the class.

▼ **Links to: Physical and health education**

Continue your discussion about the benefits and drawbacks of online gaming into physical and health education. Could you discuss the role of the IB learner profile attribute 'balanced'?

ACTIVITY: Design a computer game based around a global issue

■ ATL

Creative-thinking skills – Apply existing knowledge to generate new ideas, products or processes

▼ Links to: Design

This task could be done as an interdisciplinary piece of work between Individuals and societies and Design.

For this task you need to **design** a computer game. Your game should be designed around raising awareness about a global issue – for example pollution or human rights.

1. Write a synopsis for the game. What happens? What is the overall aim? Who are the characters? How is it played?
2. Write an **explanation** of how it would educate about a specific global issue.
3. Include illustrations or storyboards to help show your creativity.

■ **Figure 1.18** Computer game characters

! Take action

! Consider the ways that global brands are promoting ethical practices, such as sustainability, within their approach to the selling of goods. Launch a class discussion on ethics. What do good decisions look like? Which companies demonstrate these approaches in your opinion?

ACTIVITY: An evaluation and reflection on globalization

■ ATL

- Critical-thinking skills – Evaluate evidence and arguments
- Reflection skills – Consider content

In this task you need to create an evaluation of globalization based on your studies of the concept in this chapter. The following analytical tools will help you to complete this process.

Firstly, the 5Ws can be used to give an overview of the term:
- What is globalization?
- Where does it take place?
- Who does it affect?
- Why has it happened?
- When did the process begin/speed up?

Secondly, you could do a SWOT analysis of globalization. Use this table as a template to help to organize your ideas:

STRENGTHS	WEAKNESSES
OPPORTUNITIES	THREATS

Finally, you could further divide your ideas into the social, economic and cultural effects of globalization.

For example the impact on language can be seen as a cultural effect of globalization; the effect on entertainment can be seen as a social effect.

Put together your **evaluation** in a format appropriate for the task, such as a poster, presentation or a piece of writing.

◆ Assessment opportunities

In this activity you have practised skills that are assessed using Criterion A: Knowing and understanding (strands i and ii), Criterion C: Communicating (strands i, ii and iii) and Criterion D: Thinking critically (strands i and ii).

Reflection

In this chapter, we have explored the causes and consequences of globalization. Our case studies have looked at some of the social, cultural and economic consequences of the process of globalization. We have reflected on the benefits and drawbacks of globalization and considered how the process will affect the world in the future.

Use this table to reflect on your own learning in this chapter.					
Questions we asked	Answers we found	Any further questions now?			
Factual: What is globalization? What are transnational corporations? How has globalization affected sport? How has globalization affected the gaming industry?					
Conceptual: What are the causes of globalization? How has globalization affected language?					
Debatable: Is globalization new? Is there such a thing as a global culture?					
Approaches to learning you used in this chapter	Description – what new skills did you learn?	How well did you master the skills?			
		Novice	Learner	Practitioner	Expert
Communication skills					
Reflection skills					
Information literacy skills					
Critical-thinking skills					
Creative-thinking skills					
Learner profile attribute(s)	Reflect on the importance of being caring for your learning in this chapter.				
Caring					

1   How has globalization shaped the world?

Systems | Sustainability | Identities and relationships

2 Why are natural environments important to individuals and societies?

○ The **relationships** between living things in different environments can be viewed as a **system**, and **sustainability** can help these environments to last into the future.

■ Figure 2.1 A family of bears creating a road block

CONSIDER THESE QUESTIONS:

Factual: What are biomes and where can they be found? How does climate affect the make-up of a biome? How is climate represented on a graph? How is climate change affecting the natural environments of the world?

Conceptual: How do different environments work as systems? What impact have humans had on different environments? How can sustainability help different environments?

Debatable: Should humans protect natural environments at all costs?

Now **share and compare** your thoughts and ideas with your partner, or with the whole class.

○ IN THIS CHAPTER, WE WILL …
- **Find out** about different environments in the world and how they can be seen as a system.
- **Explore** examples of the human impact on environments with case studies of grassland and rainforest biomes.
- **Take action** by promoting sustainable development both in local and global contexts.

24   Individuals and Societies for the IB MYP 2: *by Concept*

■ **These Approaches to Learning (ATL) skills will be useful …**

- Communication skills
- Organization skills
- Information literacy skills
- Critical-thinking skills
- Creative-thinking skills
- Transfer skills

● **We will reflect on this learner profile attribute …**

- **Balanced** – by exploring the importance of balance within natural environments and in connection with sustainability.

◆ **Assessment opportunities in this chapter:**

- **Criterion A**: Knowing and understanding
- **Criterion B**: Investigating
- **Criterion C**: Communicating
- **Criterion D**: Thinking critically

SEE–THINK–WONDER

Look at Figure 2.1:
- What do you see?
- What do you think about that?
- What does it make you wonder?

■ **Figure 2.2** Deserts are a type of biome. What is the climate like in a desert?

The world is full of different natural environments that affect the experience of living there. From deserts to rainforests, natural environments determine the different animal and plant life that can be found in specific places as well as how humans adapt or modify their lives to the environment. For example, the life of someone in the far north of Canada could not be more different from that of someone who lives on a tropical island.

In this chapter, we will explore examples of the different environments that exist in the world, studying how they work and why they are different. We will also consider the human impact on these environments.

THINK–PAIR–SHARE

How do you think humans have adapted to live in the following environments?

- A hot desert
- A rainforest

How might advances in technology make it easier for humans to live in harsher climates? With a partner, brainstorm a range of examples and share your ideas with the class.

KEY WORDS

climate	food chain
deforestation	global warming

2 Why are natural environments important to individuals and societies?

What are biomes and where can they be found?

Biomes are very large areas in the world that have similar vegetation, climate and animal life. There are many different ways of classifying biomes. Biomes can be based on land or in water; they can be grasslands or forests, mountains or deserts.

Similar types of biomes occur in different parts of the world, for example desert biomes can be found in Africa, Asia, Oceania and North America. Biomes are important because they provide an indication of the climate, vegetation and animal life and how different types of life have adapted to live in these areas.

In this chapter, we will be focusing on land biomes (also known as terrestrial biomes), but it is important to remember the significance of biomes that are based in water. Given the fact that around 70% of the planet's surface is water, this is very important to the planet. These aquatic biomes contain a huge range of plant and animal life.

■ **Figure 2.3** Marine biomes hold a rich diversity of life. This picture shows a kelp forest as well as shoals of fish. Marine biomes occur in the seas and oceans. Freshwater biomes include lakes, rivers and wetland areas

> **DISCUSS**
>
> What are the different ways that humans affect marine and freshwater biomes?

ACTIVITY: Create a new inquiry on marine and freshwater biomes

■ ATL

Critical-thinking skills – Formulate factual, topical, conceptual and debatable questions

Although not discussed in this book, marine and freshwater biomes can make a rich exploration for inquiry. In small groups, generate a **list** of questions that you would like to explore to find out more about these types of biomes. Once you have created a list, categorise them into factual, conceptual and debatable questions.

ACTIVITY: Where are the world's biomes?

■ ATL

Information literacy skills – Access information to be informed and to inform others

1 **Using** an atlas, write down which biome you would be living in if you lived in the following cities:
   - Cairo
   - Auckland
   - Jakarta
   - Lhasa
   - Buenos Aires
2 **Using** the map, can you spot any patterns for the locations of the different biomes? **Explain** why you think this might be.
3 Can you **identify** where you live and which biome you live in?

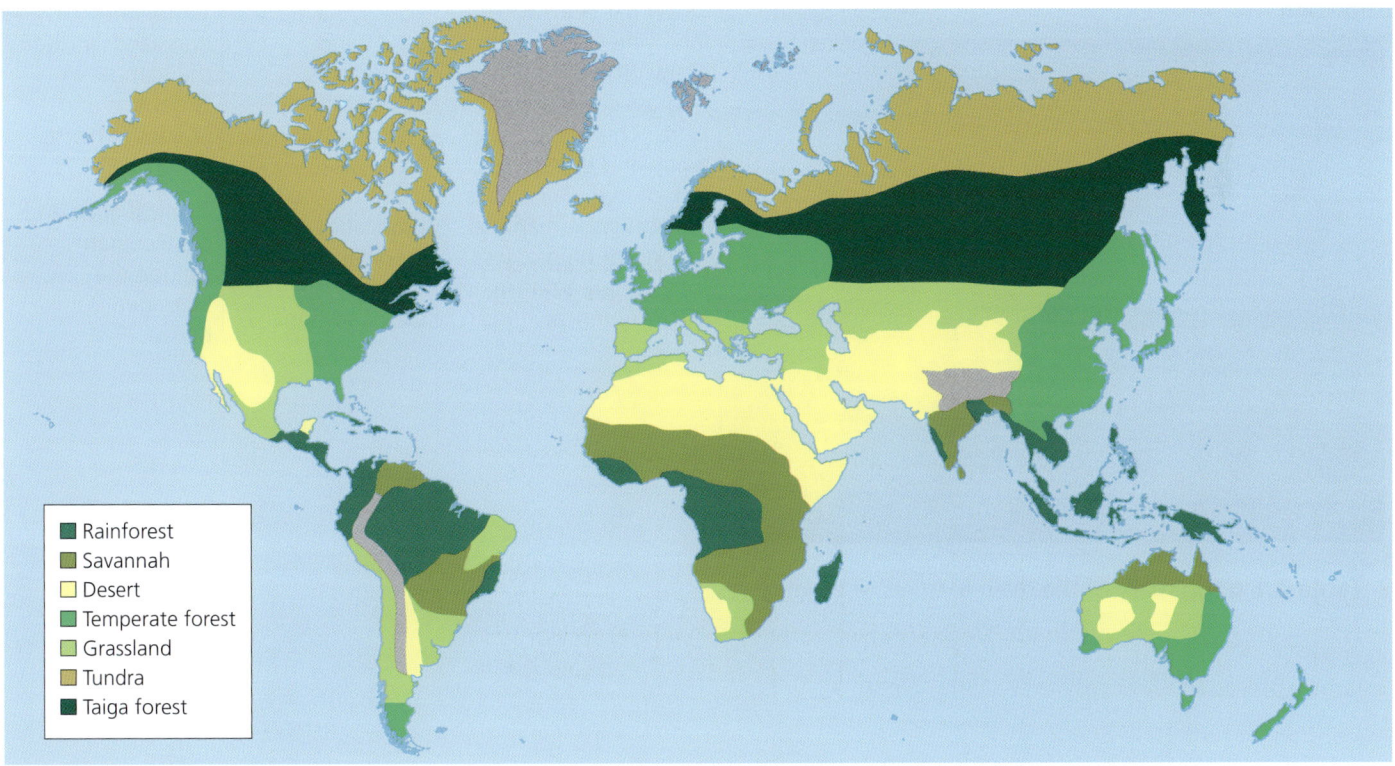

■ **Figure 2.4** Map showing the location of biomes around the world

Biome	What it looks like	Climate	Examples
Desert	Barren places that are defined by a lack of precipitation. Hot and cold deserts exist in the world. They usually lack vegetation and there is limited animal life due to their inhospitable nature. Many animals live underground during the day to escape the heat of the sun.	Dry, little rainfall through the year. Hot deserts have very high summer temperatures and mild winters. Cold deserts can also be very hot in the summer months but very cold in the winter.	Hot deserts include the Sahara Desert in North Africa and the Empty Quarter in the southern section of the Arabian Peninsula. Cold deserts include the Gobi Desert in Mongolia. Antarctica can also be seen as a polar desert due to its lack of precipitation.
Grassland	Often flat lands with low-lying vegetation. Many different types of grass cover these lands. There is a lack of woodland due to the lack of rain. Grasslands support large mammals that graze on grasses, for example bison in North America.	Usually have a wet and dry season. Temperate grasslands tend to be drier than tropical grasslands. Tropical grasslands are called savannahs.	Temperate grasslands include the Pampas in Argentina and Prairies in North America. Tropical grassland or savannah include the Serengeti in Kenya.

■ **Table 2.1** A summary of the main features of biomes

Biome	What it looks like	Climate	Examples
Tundra	Above the tree line, the tundra is covered in ice and snow through the long winter months, while during the short summer the tundra sees the growth of grasses and many different flowers. The melting ice creates a boggy terrain and there is a permanent layer of frost and ice called permafrost under the ground. A small number of animals live in the tundra including the arctic hare and caribou.	Very cold climate with low levels of precipitation. Temperatures stay in minus degrees Celsius for most of the year.	Northern parts of Russia and Canada.
Rainforest	Dense forest with a very wide variety of animals, especially insects and amphibians. Trees and vegetation compete for sunlight.	Hot and wet all year round, not much variation in temperature and precipitation levels, though there can be wet and dry seasons.	Amazon forests in South America, the Congo Basin forests in Africa.

2 Why are natural environments important to individuals and societies?

How does climate affect the make-up of a biome?

The make-up of biomes is determined by a range of factors, but perhaps the most important is **climate**.

Climate is the term used to describe the average or typical weather of a particular location. Climate gives us an idea of what the weather is usually like at a particular time of the year. Climate determines what a biome looks like as the amount of precipitation and temperature affect what can grow in a particular location to support animal life.

Climate is determined by a number of factors.

LATITUDE

An important factor is the **latitude** of a particular location. Locations at latitude 0°, the equator, experience hot weather all year round, as well as plentiful rain in areas of rainforest. Locations at latitudes that are in the far north or south of the planet experience more inhospitable climates given their lack of exposure to the Sun for large parts of the year.

■ **Figure 2.5** Diagram showing the effect of latitude on the appearance of different biomes

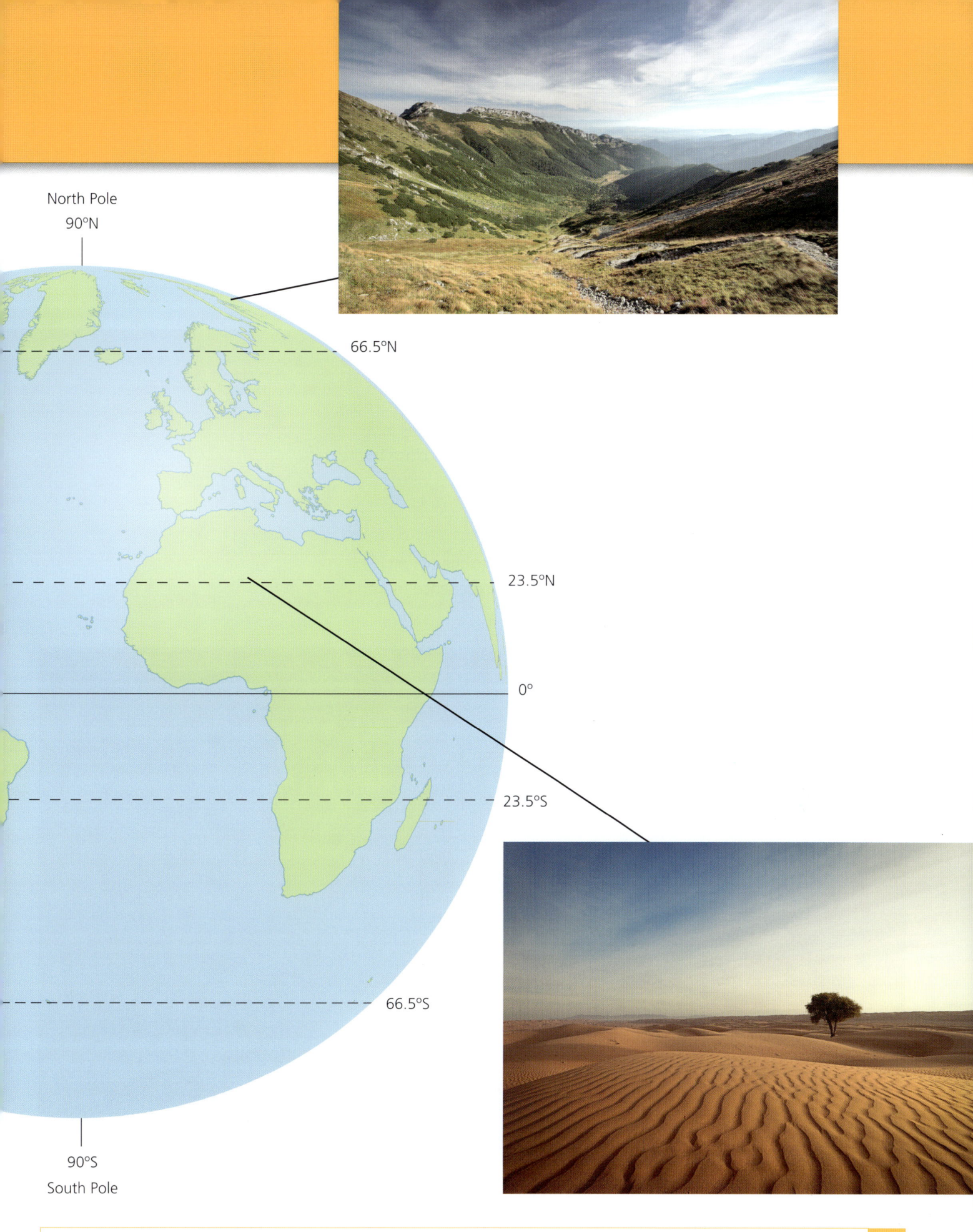

2 Why are natural environments important to individuals and societies?

DISTANCE FROM THE SEA

Another factor is the distance from the sea. The sea has a significant effect on the climate of a particular location as it can have a cooling effect during times of hot weather and a warming effect in times of cold weather. This is called the **maritime effect** and explains some of the differences in climate between locations on the same line of latitude that are close to the sea and those that are not.

ALTITUDE

Altitude is also an important consideration. This refers to the height above sea level. High locations in tropical climates can experience more temperate climates due to their higher altitude.

■ **Figure 2.6** The peak of Chimborazo in Ecuador is snow capped, even though it is close to the equator

OCEAN CURRENTS

Another factor that can warm a particular location is **ocean currents**. For example, the Gulf Stream warms certain areas of Western Europe, meaning that they have more temperate climates than other areas of the same latitude.

■ **Figure 2.7** Luskentyre is in the Outer Hebrides, an area of Scotland affected by the Gulf Stream

How is climate represented on a graph?

Figure 2.8 Buenos Aires, Argentina

The climate of a location can be recorded using a climate graph. This shows the average temperature and precipitation in each month. Take a look at the climate graphs for Buenos Aires and Medan.

MONTH	JAN	FEB	MAR	APR	MAY	JUN	JUL	AUG	SEP	OCT	NOV	DEC
Average temperature, °C	23.6	22.8	20.6	16.4	13.5	11	10.6	11.5	13.5	16.4	19.5	22
Average Precipitation, mm	104	98	115	97	80	61	59	63	68	104	98	93

Table 2.2 Climate data for Buenos Aires, Argentina

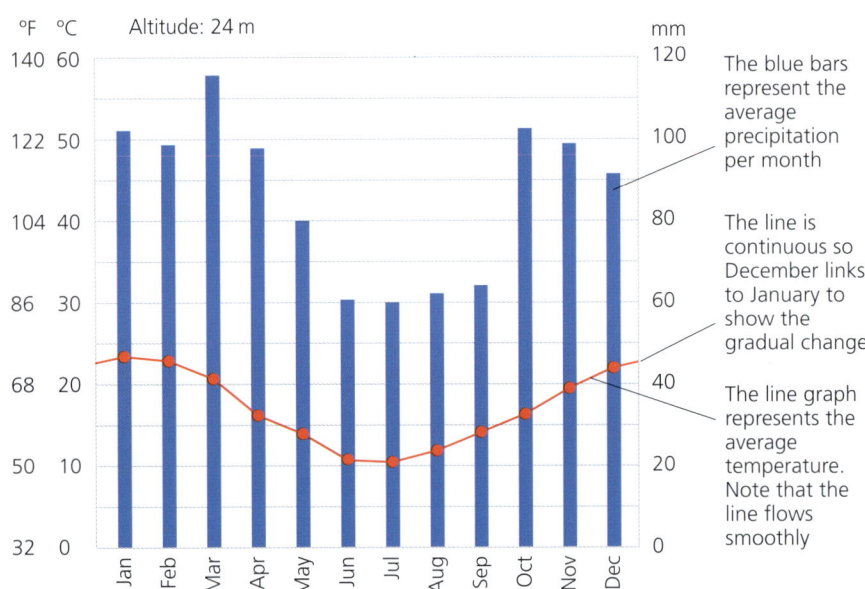

The blue bars represent the average precipitation per month

The line is continuous so December links to January to show the gradual change

The line graph represents the average temperature. Note that the line flows smoothly

Figure 2.9 Climate graph for Buenos Aires, Argentina – an example of a city in a grassland biome

MONTH	JAN	FEB	MAR	APR	MAY	JUN	JUL	AUG	SEP	OCT	NOV	DEC
Average temperature, °C	26.1	26.4	26.9	27.2	27.5	27.3	27	27.1	26.8	26.7	26.2	26
Average precipitation, mm	112	90	97	158	180	145	155	197	255	285	256	207

■ **Table 2.3** Climate data for Medan, Indonesia

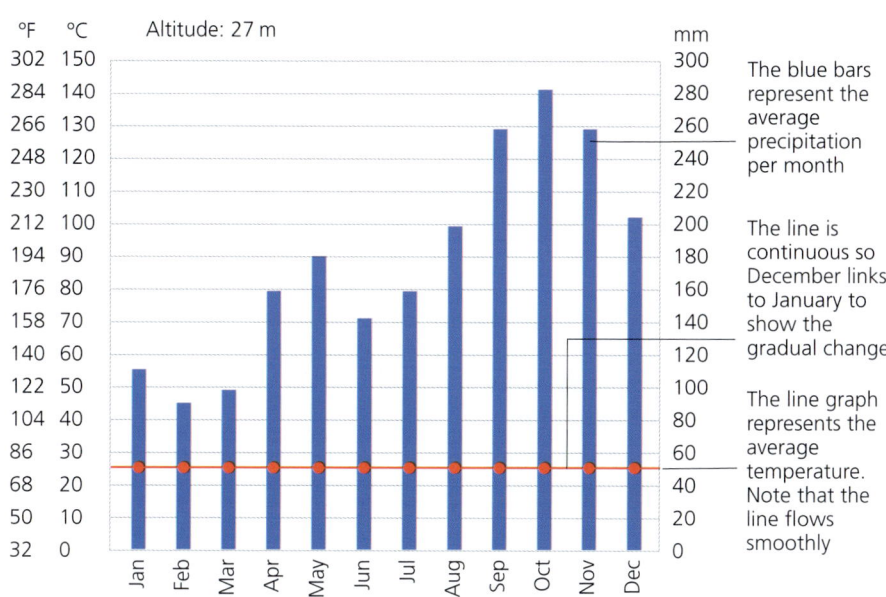

■ **Figure 2.10** Climate graph for Medan, Indonesia – an example of a city in a rainforest biome

■ **Figure 2.11** Downtown Medan, Indonesia

2   Why are natural environments important to individuals and societies?

ACTIVITY: Interpreting and constructing climate graphs

ATL

- Critical-thinking skills – Interpret data
- Organization skills – Use appropriate strategies for organizing complex information

Use the information in the graphs, photos and tables on pages 34–35 to answer the following questions.

1 Find the following:
   a the hottest month of the year in Buenos Aires
   b the driest month of the year in Buenos Aires
   c the wettest month of the year in Medan
   d the coldest month of the year in Medan
2 **Calculate** the overall average temperature and average precipitation for Buenos Aires for the entire year.
3 Denny, a friend of yours, is planning a short holiday to Buenos Aires in March. Write Denny a short letter **explaining** what to expect in terms of weather at this time of the year. Include details about the clothes he should take to be well prepared for visiting the city at this time of the year.
4 Medan is in a rainforest biome. Using the climate data, **explain** why rainforests would be able to grow in the area where Medan is located.
5 **Construct** a climate graph for Riyadh in Saudi Arabia. When you have constructed the graph for Riyadh, write two paragraphs to **describe** the overall climate of the city. Within your response **explain** what biome you think Riyadh is in and why.

MONTH	JAN	FEB	MAR	APR	MAY	JUN	JUL	AUG	SEP	OCT	NOV	DEC
Average temperature, °C	14.3	16.8	21.4	25.7	31.3	33.6	34.7	32.6	31.8	26.6	20.6	15.7
Average precipitation, mm	16	7	29	29	10	0	0	0	0	1	7	12

■ Table 2.4 Climate data for Riyadh, Saudi Arabia

◆ Assessment opportunities

This activity can be assessed using Criterion C: Communicating (strands i and ii) and Criterion D: Thinking critically (strands i and ii).

Constructing climate graphs

Climate graphs require you to show two sets of data: average temperature and average precipitation. Temperature should be plotted as a line graph and precipitation should be plotted as a bar chart. You need to ensure that your vertical axes are numbered so that the graph will be presented to a high standard. The points plotted for precipitation and temperature should fall into the middle of each month column. Connect your line graph with a smooth line and remember that the line from December should be at a similar level to that for January. Use the examples in the book to help you to construct these graphs. You can find more climate data at the following site to construct more climate graphs: http://en.climate-data.org/

DISCUSS

Discuss in pairs how the following features would affect climate and then copy and complete the table.

Feature	How would it affect climate?
Latitude	
Distance from the sea	
Altitude	
Ocean currents	

How do different environments work as systems?

UNDERSTANDING ECOSYSTEMS

Within biomes, there are many different examples of **ecosystems**. Ecosystems are communities of living organisms within a specific environment that are interdependent. For example, a small pond will have an ecosystem within it made up of plants and animals that have relationships with each other. Ecosystems vary in size tremendously and can be found in:

- A pond
- A cave
- An area of woodland
- A forest
- An ocean

Different living organisms within an ecosystem can be labelled to show their function. The following terms are useful for understanding the relationships within an ecosystem.

Producers

Producers are the plants and vegetation within the ecosystem. Their type and quantity depends on the location of the ecosystem. They provide food for the consumers. Producers grow using sunlight, water and nutrients from the ground.

Consumers

Consumers are the different species of animals within an ecosystem. They feed on plants (herbivore), animals (carnivore) or both (omnivore). Consumers can be split into two further categories of **primary** and **secondary**. Primary consumers are typically herbivores that feed off the plants while secondary consumers are usually carnivores that feed off the primary consumers. In a food web the number of consumers can increase until you reach the **apex predator(s)** that is effectively at the top of the food chain and is not preyed upon by other animals. There may be more than one type of apex predator in competition with each other for prey.

Scavengers

Scavengers are opportunist animals and birds that feed off the bodies of dead animals. They often begin the process of breaking down dead animals before the decomposers finish. Examples include vultures and wild dogs.

Decomposers

Decomposers are responsible for the breaking down of dead animals and plants. For example, mushrooms and some insects feed on decaying matter. This matter then forms into nutrients in the ground to help the growth of plants and trees.

> ### DISCUSS
> Do you think that the relationships within an ecosystem always stay the same? In what circumstances would they change? What do you understand by the term 'interdependence' and how do ecosystems help us to understand this concept?

THINK–PAIR–SHARE

Take a look at the photos in Figure 2.12. With a partner, decide which term best describes their position in a food web:
- Primary consumer
- Decomposer
- Producer
- Secondary consumer

Share your answers with the class.

Figure 2.12 Where do these living things belong in a food web?

2 Why are natural environments important to individuals and societies?

FOOD WEBS

An example of a food chain within an ecosystem would typically include a producer that is eaten by a primary consumer who in turn is eaten by a secondary consumer. **Food webs** are more common, however, due to the fact that many living things within ecosystems feed on the same thing. For example, many primary consumers might eat grass within an ecosystem, or many secondary consumers might all feed off rabbits.

Figure 2.13 shows part of a food web within the African savannah, an example of a tropical grassland.

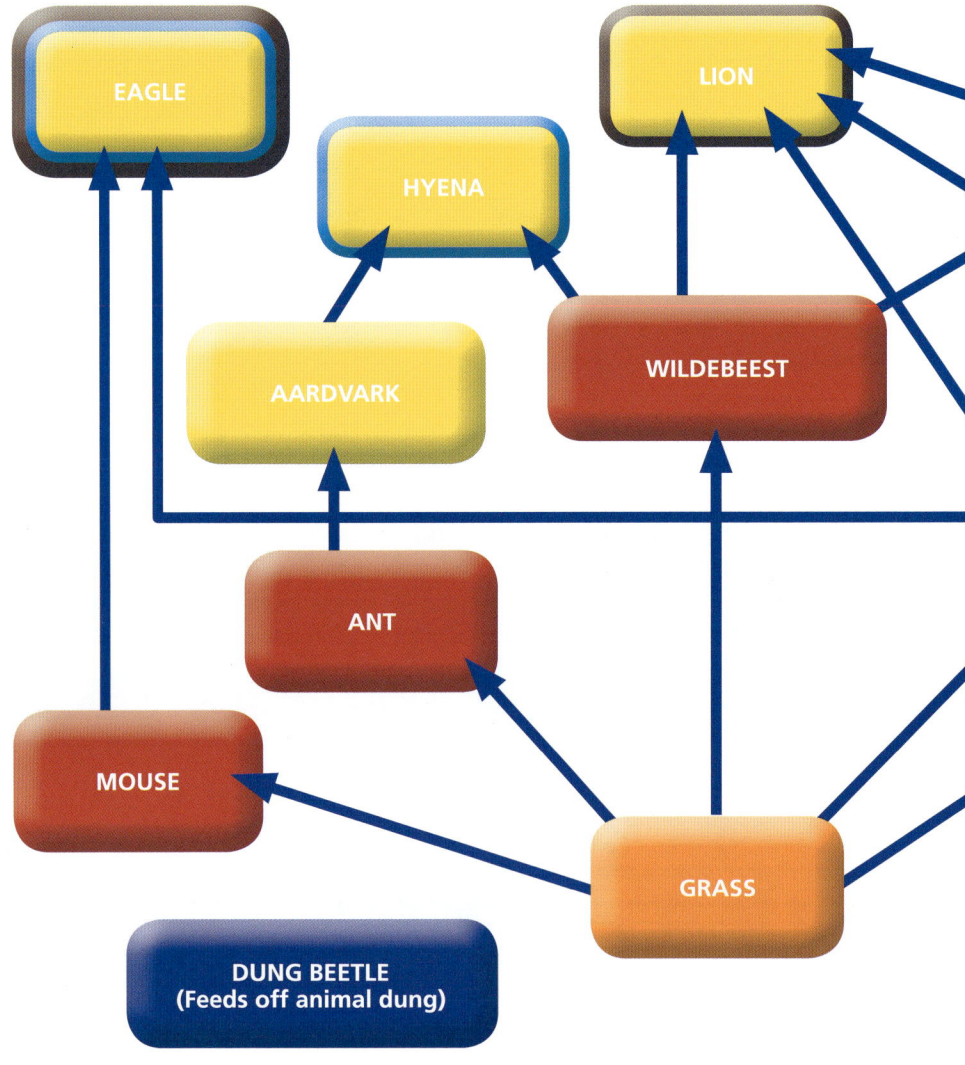

■ **Figure 2.13** Diagram of a food web

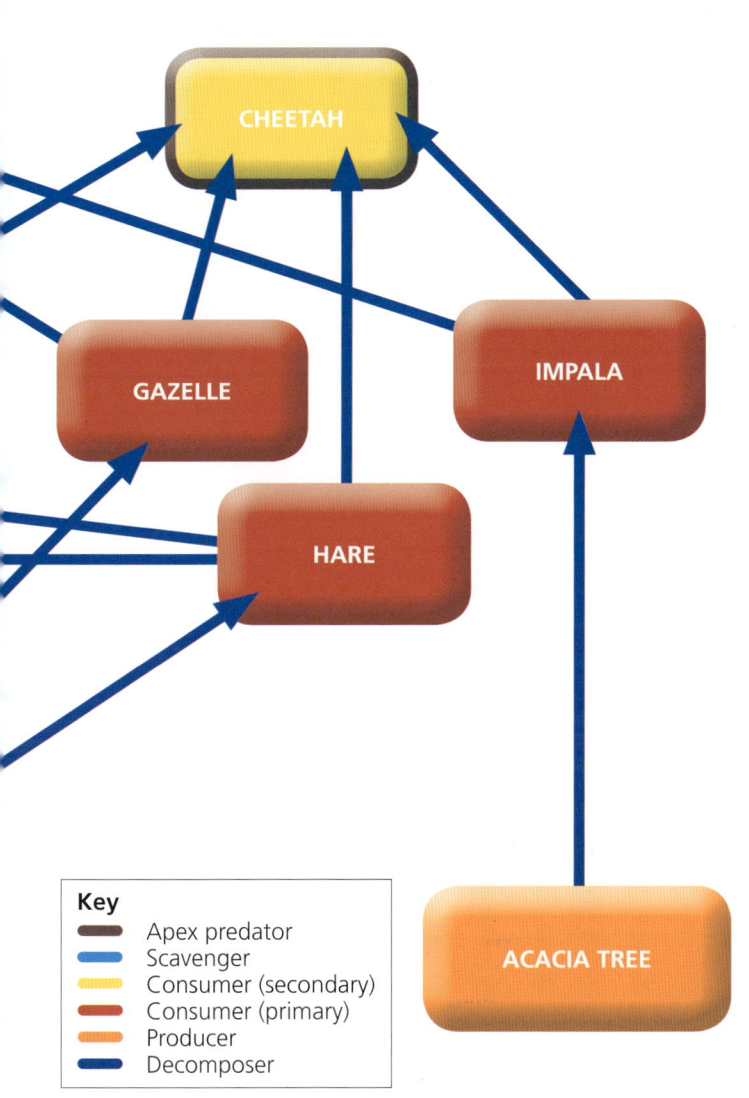

ACTIVITY: Food webs

■ ATL

Information literacy skills – Access information to be informed and to inform others

Look at the food web in Figure 2.13 and answer the following questions.

1. Why do you think the eagle could be described as both a scavenger and an apex predator?
2. What role does the dung beetle play in this ecosystem?
3. What would happen if you took the aardvark out of the web?
4. Imagine there was a fire that destroyed the grass and acacia trees. How might the ecosystem be affected?
5. Choose one of the animals from the web and write a paragraph or, if you are feeling creative, a poem, to **describe** life on the savannah from their perspective. **Use** the diagram to help you.
6. Choose a different type of ecosystem, for example the rainforest or tundra, to **explore**. Research it and create your own food web to show the relationships within it.

◆ Assessment opportunities

In this activity you have practised skills that are assessed using Criterion A: Knowing and understanding (strands i and ii), Criterion C: Communicating (strand ii) and Criterion D: Thinking critically (strand ii).

2 Why are natural environments important to individuals and societies?

What impact have humans had on different environments?

CASE STUDY: A GRASSLAND BIOME – AGRICULTURE IN THE PAMPAS IN SOUTH AMERICA

The Pampas is a large area of grassland found in Argentina, Uruguay and a small section of Brazil. It is a large area of mostly flat land covered in grasses. There is a distinct lack of trees in this area, as the Pampas is subject to regular fires that make it difficult for trees to take root and grow here. Grass, on the other hand, can grow back very quickly after fires and so is permanently a feature of this biome. The Pampas has a rich biodiversity. There are many different species of grass in these areas as well as a range of birds and mammals. These different life forms have adapted to the dry and humid climate of the Pampas.

The human impact on the Pampas region has been mainly through the use of land for agriculture. In the past this has included large amounts of cattle ranching. Cattle ranching has been a feature of the Pampas for centuries and accounts for Argentina's best-known export – beef. Argentine beef is famous around the world for its quality. The Pampas is also home to the **gaucho**, the South American cowboy or cowgirl who has traditionally worked these lands.

However, the traditional farming methods have changed in recent years to make way for more large-scale farming and industrial methods to bring about greater production levels. This is particularly relevant to the farming of soy, which is a very profitable export for the Argentine economy. The increase in soy production has been criticised for its impact on the traditional uses of the Pampas, and the intense nature of this farming is seen to be harmful to the biodiversity and quality of the soils in this area.

■ **Figure 2.14** Map showing the Pampas in South America

■ **Figure 2.15** Landscape of the Pampas

SOURCE A

Outside the town of Villegas, in the western Argentine Pampas, the land appears as a tri-colored patchwork in mid-summer. There's the deep green of corn leaves, the lighter green soybeans, and the straw colored stubble of corn stalks that have been sprayed with pesticides after harvest. That's just about it for as far as the eye can see, which in this case is far. The land is flat – it rises 25 centimeters for every kilometer as it reaches the foothills of the Andes. But if you're familiar with how this land has looked for decades, you realize there's something missing: pasture … For the better part of the last 60 years, these lands have been worked in a rotation of grass and grain, with the sun as the system's main fuel and cattle as its central engine … Yet outside Villegas, the cattle and the grass are being removed from the system. The biggest herd I saw was packed into a feedlot with capacity for 10,000 head. Across the more than 120 million acres of the Pampas, grass is being torn up and the land planted in genetically modified soy. The cattle are being pushed into feedlots or sent north and west to lands too poor to grow crops, just as happened in the U.S. corn-belt decades ago. And, as in the United States, as the cattle move out, industrial farms growing fewer and fewer crops with more and more pesticides and fertilizers are taking their place. The very nature of Pampean agriculture – which along with the gaucho myth lies at the heart of Argentine consciousness – is changing.

Nicholas Kusnetz, http://nacla.org

SOURCE B

Read this article about the loss of soil fertility in Argentina.

www.reuters.com/article/us-argentina-soils-analysis-idUSBRE99M0G120131023

Figure 2.16 A gaucho in the Pampas

ACTIVITY: The Pampas

■ **ATL**

- Information literacy skills – Access information to be informed and to inform others
- Critical-thinking skills – Develop contrary or opposing arguments

1 What type of biome is the Pampas in?
2 According to Sources A and B on page 43, why has soy production increased in the Pampas region?
3 What are some of the consequences of the increase in farming soy?
4 Who are gauchos? How do these issues affect them?
5 Let's consider the debatable question for this chapter: Should humans protect natural environments at all costs? **Discuss** this question in groups. Make connections with the Pampas case study. Write up two different arguments to show different approaches to this issue.

Figure 2.17 A gaucho

▼ Links to: Language and literature

The traditions of the gaucho can teach us about the relationship between cultural identity and natural environments. Why do you think this relationship exists? How can the natural environments that people live in affect the development of their language and culture and, more broadly, their identity and relationships? Can you think of other examples?

■ **Figure 2.18** Forests of the Congo Basin

CASE STUDY: A RAINFOREST BIOME – THE CONGO BASIN, AFRICA

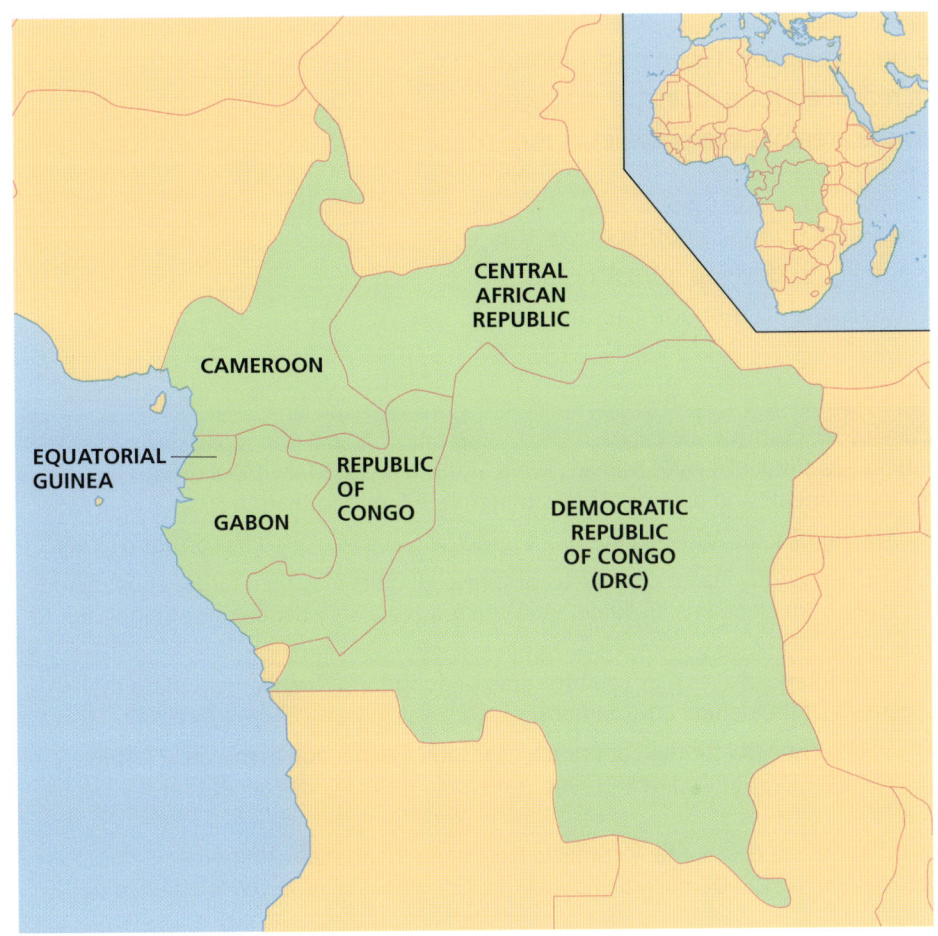

■ **Figure 2.19** The countries of the Congo Basin

The rainforests of the Congo Basin in Africa can be found in the countries of Cameroon, Gabon, Equatorial Guinea and the Central African Republic as well as the Republic of Congo and the Democratic Republic of Congo (DRC). This covers a huge area of land and is the largest rainforest in the world after the Amazon in South America. Flowing through this vast area of forest is the Congo River.

The Congo Basin has an extraordinarily rich diversity of plant and animal life, with many new species being discovered all the time. For example, a new species of monkey, the lesula, was discovered as recently as 2007. The area is home to many endangered animals including rare species of elephants and gorillas.

■ **Figure 2.20** Elephants in the Congo Basin

The forests are very important to the world. They are sometimes described as the world's second lung after the Amazon, because of the huge quantities of carbon they take out of the atmosphere. Protecting these forests is therefore an important step to prevent **climate change** in the future. However, there are many resources in the Congo Basin that people want to access in order to generate profits. These include the trees and the minerals and precious metals that lie under the ground of the forests.

The issues affecting the Congo Basin are quite complex. Given its ecological and environmental importance, there is a real need for sustainable practices to keep the forests healthy. Unfortunately the area has seen conflict in the past which has restricted development of such practices.

The Democratic Republic of Congo has experienced much conflict over the years, significantly affecting the country's ability to develop infrastructure and systems to help the people who live there and to manage the natural resources sustainably.

Issue	Why is this a problem?
Deforestation	The loss of trees causes habitat loss for wildlife and humans living in these areas. Many tribal groups live in harmony with their natural environments and deforestation is therefore a threat to them.
Mining	Mining usually requires the clearing of trees. Workers are often underpaid and exploited by corrupt officials.
Road building	Road building provides access to previously inaccessible areas of forest. Hunters may then target endangered species for their profits, e.g. ivory from elephants. In some areas the roads are very dangerous at night due to bandits targeting vehicles.
Political instability	The continued instability of governments makes it difficult to establish long-term development plans that work for sustainable management of the natural environment.
International interest in resources	International companies have been criticised for their approach to resource extraction in this area. Often short-term profits are prioritised over long-term development that would have a wider benefit for the people who live in the region.
Conflict	Conflict inevitably leads to suffering and death. Many conflicts have been associated with border disagreements and access to resources. The Democratic Republic of Congo has been severely affected by conflict for many years.

■ **Table 2.5** Issues affecting the Congo Basin

Figure 2.21 Soldiers in the Democratic Republic of Congo

DISCUSS: Historical inquiry

1. How do you think the following historical processes would affect natural environments?
   - Warfare, e.g. Vietnam War, First World War
   - Industrialization, e.g. Industrial Revolution in Britain during the 19th century
   - Urban growth, e.g. development of megacities of over 10 million people
2. Can you think of any processes or developments that have helped natural environments?

EXTENSION

Colonialism and the Congo Basin

Figure 2.22 'In the rubber coils', a political cartoon about the rule of King Leopold

Colonialism is a process by which one country takes control of other parts of the world politically and economically.

During the 19th century, most of Africa was under the colonial control of a small number of European countries. The forests of the Congo Basin came under the control of the Belgian king, Leopold II.

He founded the Congo Free State in the late 19th century with initial intentions to improve the lives of the people, but then exploited the people and the natural wealth of the area. This included the accumulation of ivory and the selling of rubber to markets around the world. Local people did not benefit from this and many people were exploited and died during this time. This had a long-lasting negative effect on the area.

2   Why are natural environments important to individuals and societies?

ACTIVITY: Circle of perspectives

Consider the issues facing the Congo Basin.

1. In groups, take on one of the following perspectives:
    - Spokesperson for an indigenous tribe from an undisturbed area of the forest
    - The owner of an international mining company
    - An activist from an environmental group based in the area
    - A worker for a logging company from Kinshasa in the Democratic Republic of Congo
    - A United Nations specialist in sustainable development
    - A government official
2. Research your character and the issues facing the Congo Basin, and then **discuss** the issues as a group, taking on the role of your character.
3. The group should **discuss** this question: 'How can we help the Congo Basin region to develop sustainably?'
4. Reflect – write a reflection based on this activity. What did you learn from the different perspectives? What were the challenges? Can you reflect on any solutions to these issues?

■ Figure 2.23 Circle of perspectives

How is climate change affecting the natural environments of the world?

One of the biggest challenges facing the world at present is climate change. Within the scientific community there is broad consensus that climate change is a major global issue that needs to be taken seriously by all nations in the world. Specific concerns have been raised over the following issues:
- Melting ice
- Rising sea levels
- Increases in extreme weather events
- Disruption of biomes

In 2015 the United Nations Climate Change Conference took place in Paris. Commitments were made to reduce global warming by limiting greenhouse gas emissions.

SOURCE A

Read the final paragraph of the article by climate scientist and retired astronaut Piers J. Sellers.

www.nytimes.com/2016/01/17/opinion/sunday/cancer-and-climate-change.html

SOURCE B

■ Figure 2.24 Cartoon on the issue of climate change

SOURCE C

Read the penultimate paragraph of the article by climate scientist and retired astronaut Piers J. Sellers, beginning 'What should the rest of us do?'.

www.nytimes.com/2016/01/17/opinion/sunday/cancer-and-climate-change.html

SOURCE D

'I Was Born Into A World' by James Franco

I was born into a world
Before recycling was a thing,
Before oil wars,
When the biggest world
Threat was nuclear.
The only extinct thing
Was the Dodo,
We consumed and junked.
Then we were told about
Droughts, and disappearing
Rainforests.
About melting ice caps,
And we fought Iraq
For a second time,
Like father like son,
We needed our oil
Because we didn't want
Those electric cars.
At one time there were
Huge monsters that
Walked where we walk,
Nature swallowed them easy.
Or maybe you believe
It all started with Adam and Eve,
But they too were kicked
From the garden
As are we,
With our poison beaches
Run down towns
And our atmosphere
That kills.
I write a poem
And preach to the converted.
We send out loud messages
To ourselves,
That our world is dying: 1984,
Blade Runner,
Armageddon, The Road.
I've yet to read a book,
Or watch a film about a future
I'd like to live in.
Fortunately for me,
I'll die before the earth,
But I'd like a place for my
Computer chip self
To click and beep
In bright, clean happiness.

ACTIVITY: Climate change

ATL

- Information literacy skills – Make connections between various sources of information
- Creative-thinking skills – Use brainstorming and visual diagrams to generate new ideas and inquiries

1. What is climate change? What impact do you think it has/will have on natural environments?
2. What is the message of Source B?
3. According to the poem in Source D, what are some of the ways that humans have negatively affected the environments of the world? The author of the poem is a famous film actor. How can celebrities help to raise awareness about global issues?
4. Read Sources A and C. Why might the perspective of an astronaut be particularly useful to understanding climate change? What is the message of the article?
5. In groups, brainstorm the different ways that human society can a) help reduce the impact of climate change, b) prepare for it.
6. Dig deeper. Research climate change further and put together a class project on the topic.

Assessment opportunities

In this activity you have practised skills that are assessed using Criterion D: Thinking critically (strand ii).

How can sustainability help different environments?

One way that natural environments can be supported and maintained is through more sustainable uses of land and resources. This means that there is planning involved to ensure that the environments will remain intact into the future.

ACTIVITY: Sustainability in practice

ATL

Transfer skills – Apply skills and knowledge in unfamiliar situations

Take a look at the following scenarios. **Explain** why each of these would help to sustain the natural environments of the world.

- **Reforestation** – planting new trees to replace those lost by fires or logging
- **Renewable resources** – using renewable resources such as water, wind and the sun to generate electricity
- **Recycling** – reusing materials such as paper and metals
- **Sustainable tourism** – creating tourist opportunities for people that have benefits for the natural environment
- **Supporting local business** – supporting local farming and fishing industries
- **Investment in public transport** – including bus and rail networks and cycling schemes
- **Protecting natural habitats from development** – such as areas of wetland

REFLECTION

Reflect further on the different ways that people can help to sustain the natural environments of the world. Consider this in local, national and global contexts.

Local	National	Global
What would sustainability look like in a local area? What sort of practices would take place? Who would be involved?	How would sustainable practices be carried out on a national scale? Who would coordinate this? What do you think some of the priorities would be?	How could sustainability be encouraged globally? What role could international business play? What are the opportunities and challenges here?

ACTIVITY: Magazine article on natural environments

ATL

Communication skills – Find information for disciplinary and interdisciplinary inquiries, using a variety of media; Organize and depict information logically

Create a magazine article on the natural environments of a country or region of your choice.

Here are some suggested case studies.

Suggested case study	Biome
Antarctica	Polar region
Iceland	Tundra and taiga forest
Namibia	Desert
Borneo	Rainforest
Mongolia	Grassland, desert
Tibet	Mountain
New Zealand	Deciduous forest

Within your article, you should consider the following:
- Where is your country or region in the world? What biome(s) would you find there?
- What is the climate like? Include data and a graph.
- What does the natural environment look like? What are the features of ecosystems in this area? What is the flora and fauna? How are they interdependent? Include diagrams and/or images.
- Provide two examples of the human impact on the area, for example mining, farming, tourism, climate change.
- Write a reflection on some of the opportunities and threats facing the natural environments in this area.

◆ Assessment opportunities

In this activity you have practised skills that are assessed using Criterion A: Knowing and understanding (strands i and ii), Criterion B: Investigating (strand iii) and Criterion C: Communicating (strands i, ii and iii).

! Take action

! Environmental sustainability begins with individuals making a difference in their local community. Find out which type of biome you live in or close to and the local environmental issues.

Reflection

In this chapter, we have explored the different natural environments that occur and how they work as systems. We have seen the delicate relationships within these environments that can be threatened by both natural hazards and human actions. Finally, we have considered the ways in which sustainable uses of these environments can help them to last into the future.

Use this table to reflect on your own learning in this chapter.						
Questions we asked	Answers we found	Any further questions now?				
Factual: What are biomes and where can they be found? How does climate affect the make-up of a biome? How is climate represented on a graph? How is climate change affecting the natural environments of the world?						
Conceptual: How do different environments work as systems? What impact have humans had on different environments? How can sustainability help different environments?						
Debatable: Should humans protect natural environments at all costs?						
Approaches to learning you used in this chapter	Description – what new skills did you learn?	How well did you master the skills?				
		Novice	Learner	Practitioner	Expert	
Communication skills						
Organization skills						
Information literacy skills						
Critical-thinking skills						
Creative-thinking skills						
Transfer skills						
Learner profile attribute(s)	Reflect on the importance of being balanced for your learning in this chapter.					
Balanced						

2 Why are natural environments important to individuals and societies?

Time, place and space | *Perspective; Identity* | *Fairness and development*

3 What was life like in the Middle Ages?

○ The **identity** and **development** of **societies of the past** can be explored through the **perspectives** of the people who lived there.

CONSIDER THESE QUESTIONS:

Factual: When was the Middle Ages? What was the impact of the decline of the Roman empire? How was society structured during the Middle Ages? What was life like in Britain during the Middle Ages? Which empires expanded their influence during the Middle Ages? What was life like in China during the Middle Ages?

Conceptual: What perspectives can be used to study the past? Why is continuity important to the study of history?

Debatable: Have the Middle Ages been misrepresented in history?

Now **share and compare** your thoughts and ideas with your partner, or with the whole class.

○ IN THIS CHAPTER, WE WILL …
- **Find out** about some of the major global developments that occurred during The Middle Ages.
- **Explore** different aspects of people's lives during the Middle Ages.
- **Take action** by finding opportunities to engage in the skills of historical research and interpretation.

■ These Approaches to Learning (ATL) skills will be useful …
- Communication skills
- Critical-thinking skills
- Creative-thinking skills

● We will reflect on this learner profile attribute …
- **Knowledgeable** – by finding opportunities to increase our understanding of the world in previous centuries.

◆ Assessment opportunities in this chapter:
- **Criterion A:** Knowing and understanding
- **Criterion B:** Investigating
- **Criterion C:** Communicating
- **Criterion D:** Thinking critically

■ **Figure 3.1** Joan of Arc

The woman pictured on the horse in Figure 3.1 is Joan of Arc – a French heroine from the Middle Ages who was famously burned at the stake towards the end of the Hundred Years War between England and France. In many ways the picture depicts some of the commonly held associations with the Middle Ages: a time of battles, vast castles and knights carrying the banners and flags of their allegiance. The Middle Ages are also thought of as a time when there was little progress, with people leading very tough lives. However, this representation does not always reflect the time period accurately as despite the difficult lives that people experienced there were also many examples of progress.

In this chapter, we will explore some of the major developments in this period of history by taking a closer look at different societies and what life was like during this time.

COLOUR–SYMBOL–IMAGE

In small groups, choose a colour, symbol and image to represent the Middle Ages from your existing knowledge. Think about your preconceived ideas about what was happening during this time period. Share your ideas with others in the class.

KEY WORDS

dynasty
census
conquest
invasion
life expectancy
mortality
plague

When were the Middle Ages?

A note about years

In this book CE and BCE will be used in reference to specific dates. BCE means 'Before Common Era' and CE means 'Common Era'.

The Middle Ages are approximately applied to the time between the years of 500CE and 1500CE. The start of this period is usually associated with the decline of the Roman empire in Western Europe, and the end is generally considered to be the start of the Renaissance in the city states of Italy. However, these dates can be interpreted differently in different areas of the world.

DISCUSS

How can timelines help us to understand the following concepts?
- Change
- Continuity

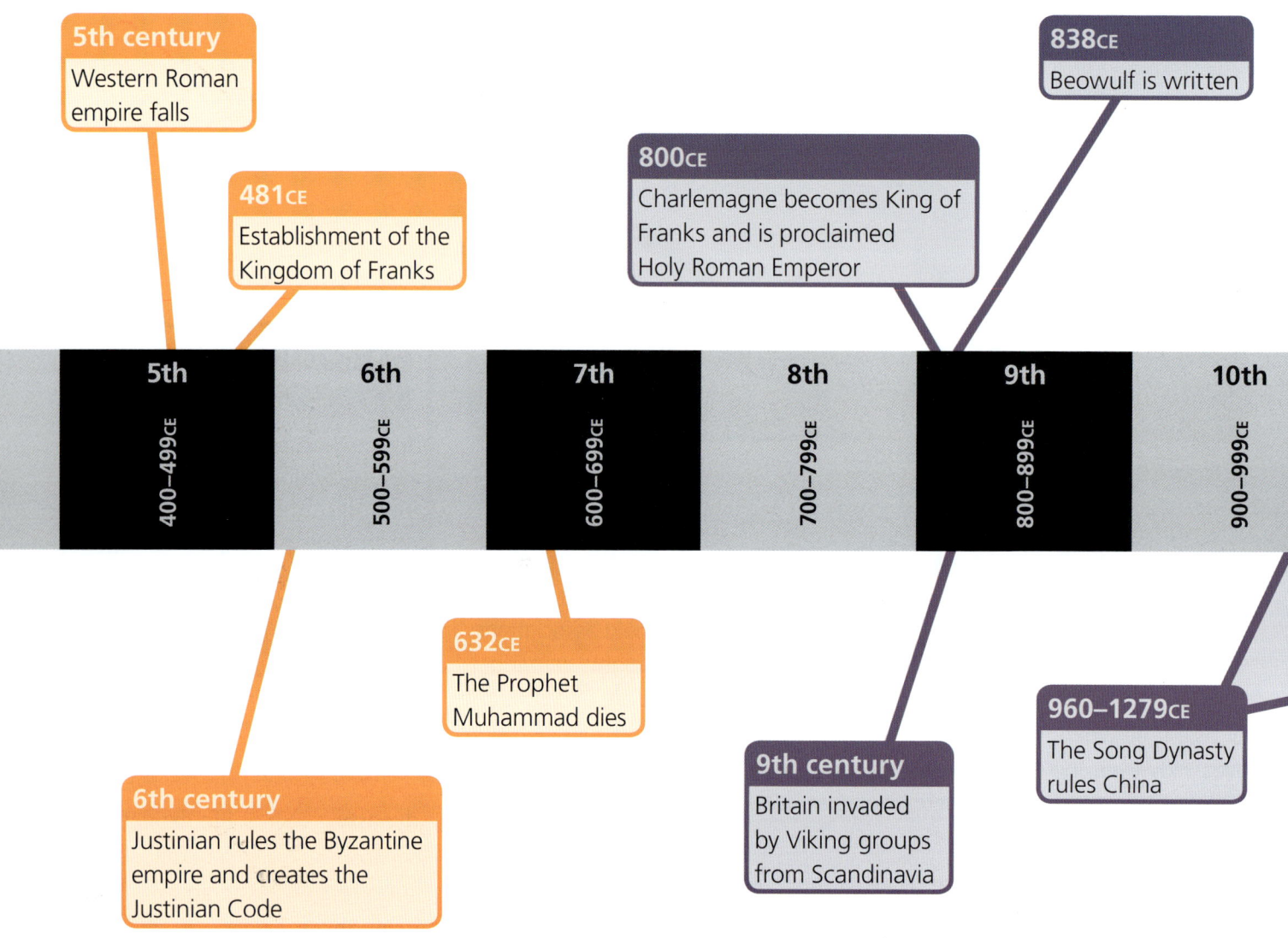

■ Figure 3.2 Timeline of the Middle Ages

WHY IS CONTINUITY IMPORTANT TO THE STUDY OF HISTORY?

Change is often studied by historians more closely than continuity as it reflects the developments that societies go through as they move forward through time. However, it is important to gain an understanding of the concept of continuity. Continuity refers to things simply staying the same. This is important when reflecting on the daily lives of people as, often, historical events may not directly affect them.

> **DISCUSS**
>
> Can you think of any examples of continuity? What sort of things always stay the same regardless of the time period that you live in? In twenty years' time, what aspects of your life do you think will be the same/different?

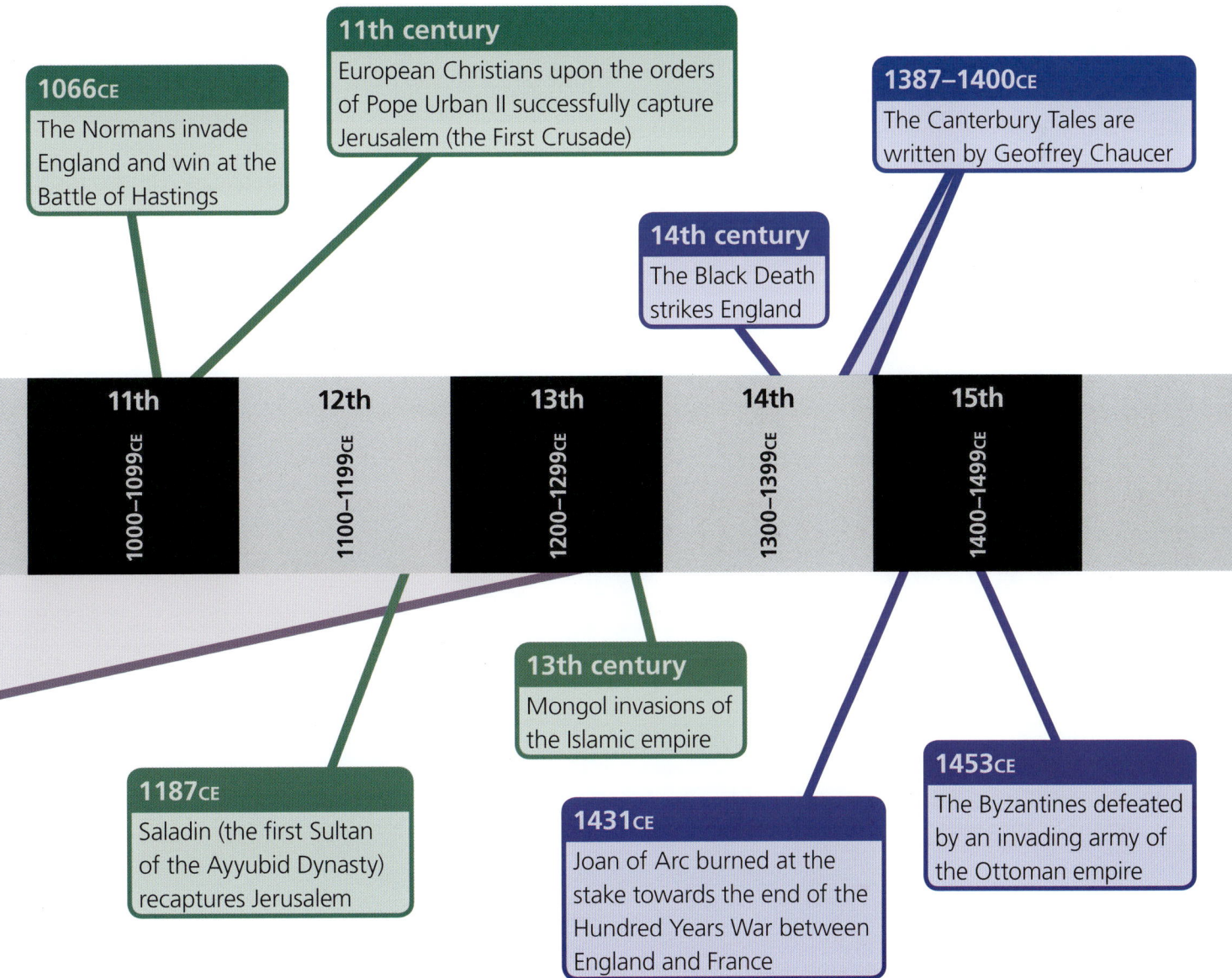

1066 CE — The Normans invade England and win at the Battle of Hastings

11th century — European Christians upon the orders of Pope Urban II successfully capture Jerusalem (the First Crusade)

1387–1400 CE — The Canterbury Tales are written by Geoffrey Chaucer

14th century — The Black Death strikes England

1187 CE — Saladin (the first Sultan of the Ayyubid Dynasty) recaptures Jerusalem

13th century — Mongol invasions of the Islamic empire

1431 CE — Joan of Arc burned at the stake towards the end of the Hundred Years War between England and France

1453 CE — The Byzantines defeated by an invading army of the Ottoman empire

Timeline:
- 11th: 1000–1099 CE
- 12th: 1100–1199 CE
- 13th: 1200–1299 CE
- 14th: 1300–1399 CE
- 15th: 1400–1499 CE

3 What was life like in the Middle Ages?

What was the impact of the decline of the Roman empire?

By 285CE the Roman empire was split in two between the Western and Eastern Roman empire. The empire had split because it had grown too large, with too many different groups to control and hold together. From this point onwards the Western half of the Roman empire gradually fell into disrepair and ruin, and was invaded by different groups across Europe, particularly Germanic tribes. The centuries following the decline of Rome in the west became known as the **Dark Ages**. For many people it represented a loss of learning and advancement as there were numerous conflicts and invasions of different groups around Europe. However, others have argued that for many people life stayed much the same after Rome fell and the term doesn't accurately reflect the time period.

The Eastern half of the Roman empire lived on as the Byzantine empire, with a new capital in Constantinople. This empire controlled lands to the east of Rome including areas of modern-day Greece, Turkey and other parts of Eastern Europe. The Byzantines successfully ruled as a continuous empire until their defeat in war to the Ottoman empire in 1453.

The city of Constantinople was established on the site of Byzantium by the emperor Constantine in the 4th century CE. The empire adopted Christianity as its religion and its language gradually shifted from Latin to Greek. A famous ruler of the Byzantine empire was Justinian. Justinian ruled during the 6th century CE and was famous for his creation of the Justinian Code: a series of laws for ruling the empire. These were based on the earlier laws of the Roman empire. He also took back territory of the Western Roman empire that had fallen under the control of different groups, including Rome. Figure 3.3 shows the extent of the empire at this time.

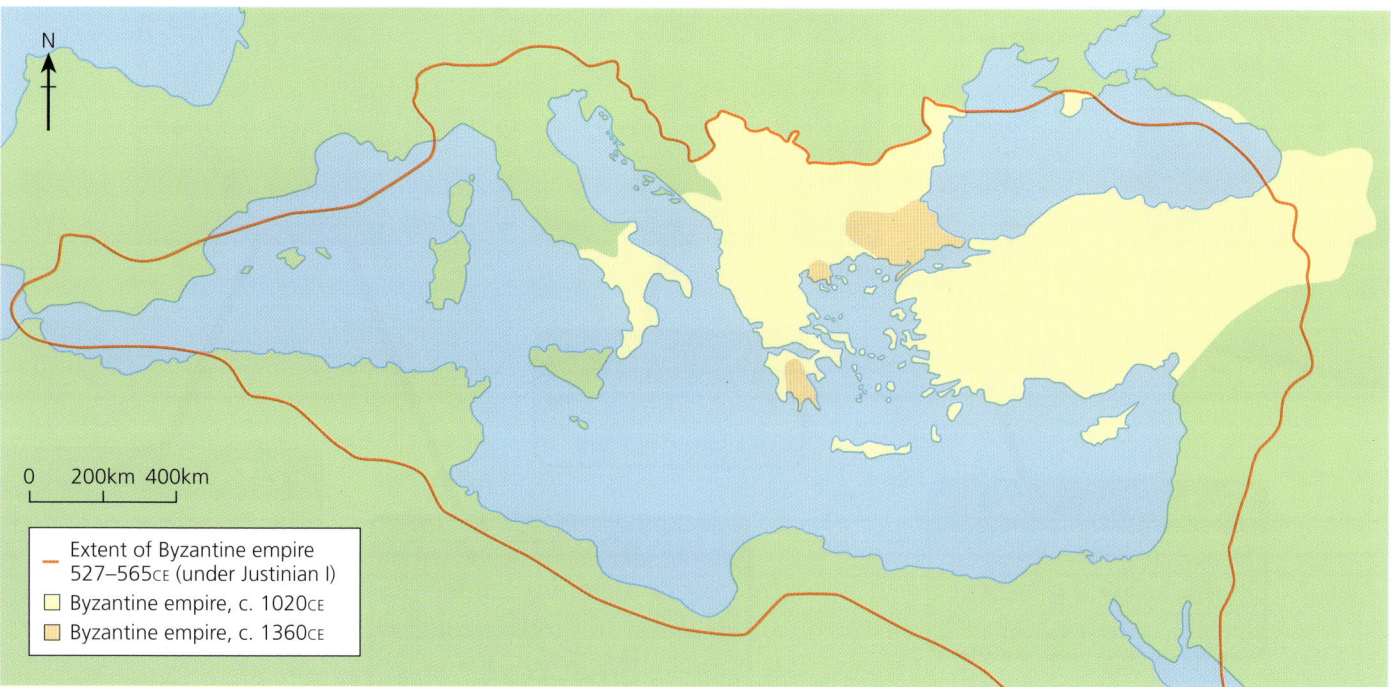

■ **Figure 3.3** Map of the Byzantine empire at different stages of history

■ **Figure 3.4** Mosaic of Justinian

■ **Figure 3.5** Illustration of Charlemagne, the Holy Roman Emperor

The Roman empire in the west of Europe did not fare as well as the Eastern Byzantine empire. There had been various attacks on the city of Rome in the 5th century and it gradually fell.

An important development in Western Europe after the fall of the Roman empire was the establishment of the Kingdom of Franks. This began under the rule of Clovis, who united the Frank people under his monarchy from 481CE. However, they really developed as a strong empire under the rule of Charlemagne who became King of Franks and from 800CE was proclaimed the Holy Roman Emperor by the Pope. Taking Christianity as its religion, this empire helped found the later monarchies of France and Germany and spread throughout Western Europe. Charlemagne is often given the nickname the 'Father of Europe' due to these achievements.

DISCUSS

Why could the decline of the Roman empire be viewed as a significant event in history?

How was society structured during the Middle Ages?

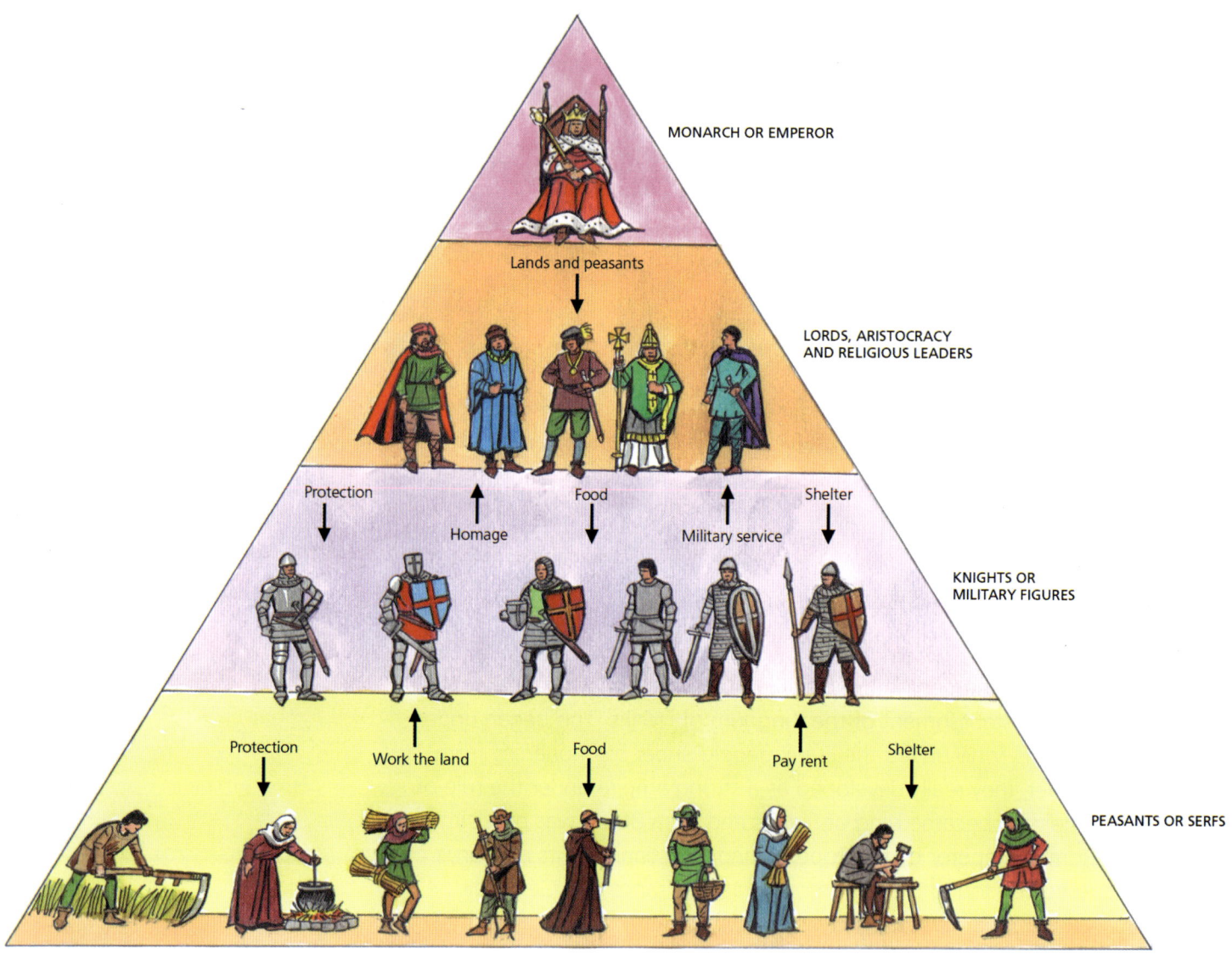

■ **Figure 3.6** The structure of the feudal system

On the whole, societies during the Middle Ages were structured using the **feudal system**. This system was developed during the 11th century by the Frank people but was used across Europe as well as in Asia and the Middle East.

Feudalism was a system of power where land was viewed as the most prized commodity. The monarch or emperor was placed at the top of the society. Underneath them there would be the lords, aristocracy and religious leaders, who were given lands and peasants to control. They supported the monarch in times of war and pledged their loyalty.

The next level down were usually the knights or military figures, who were especially important in times of war. They also paid **homage** to their lord, in the form of a public oath of loyalty.

The final group were the peasants, sometimes known as serfs. The peasants worked the land and paid rent to use this land. In return they were offered protection, food and shelter. There were variations in this system depending on where you lived. For example, in Japan, below the farmers or peasants were the merchant class and the samurai took the place of the knights.

Evaluating sources in terms of their values and limitations

When studying different sources, a useful skill is to be able to reflect upon their potential value and limitation to someone studying the topic. In Year One of the MYP, you looked at the origin and purpose of sources to think about where sources come from and what their intention is. The next step is to consider their value and limitation.

Take a look at the following guide to help you to structure your ideas for this:

- **Values** – Why would the source be useful to someone studying this topic?
- **Limitations** – What might be some of the issues that make the source less useful?

Things to consider:
- What type of source is it, for example picture, diary, history book?
- Does the source contain bias? How might this affect the value and limitation? Remember bias is often a value as well as a limitation!
- When was the source produced?
- What information does the source provide? Is the information useful to someone studying the topic?

By considering these questions, you should be able to think of some relevant values and limitations. Discussing sources in terms of their origin, purpose, value and limitation is a skill that is assessed in Criterion D: Thinking critically.

SOURCE A

■ **Figure 3.7** Painting showing serfs (peasants) giving animals to their lords as part of the feudal system

SOURCE B

Extract from Chronicles *by Jean Froissart, written in 1395 during the Hundred Years War between England and France. The book is considered to be of importance to understanding life and culture in Europe during the later stages of the Middle Ages.*

It is the custom in England, as in other countries, for the nobility to have great power over the common people, who are their serfs. This means that they are bound by law and custom to plough the fields of their masters, harvest the corn, gather it into barns, and thresh and winnow the grain; they must also mow and carry home the hay, cut and collect wood, and perform all manner of tasks of this kind.

ACTIVITY: The feudal system

■ ATL

Critical-thinking skills – Consider ideas from multiple perspectives

1 Study the diagram of the feudal system in Figure 3.6. Write three descriptions of this system using the following word counts:
   a 10–15 words
   b 30–50 words
   c 75–100 words
2 Now study Source A. What is happening in the picture?
   Consider the various perspectives. Take on the role of one of the following people in the feudal system: lord, knight, peasant or monarch. Write a paragraph to **describe** your life from that perspective. Think about your roles and responsibilities in the feudal system. Then share your ideas with others in your class who considered a different perspective from your own.
2 What does Source B suggest about the role of the peasants (serfs) in society?
   Copy and complete the following **evaluation** of the two sources (some of it has been completed already):

Source	Origin	Purpose	Value	Limitation
A	A painting from the Middle Ages			
B		Written to provide details on what Europe was like during the 14th century CE		

◆ Assessment opportunities

In this activity you have practised skills that are assessed using Criterion D: Thinking critically (strands ii, iii and iv).

REFLECTION: What perspectives can be used to study the past?

In this task we have considered different perspectives of people within the feudal system.

- What are the uses of considering different perspectives when you study a particular time period?
- What other perspectives could we consider?
- If someone from the future was studying the time period in which you lived, which perspectives do you think would be useful for them to find out what life was like?

What was life like in Britain during the Middle Ages?

INVASIONS

By the 5th century CE, the Romans had left Britain. For the next few centuries Britain was invaded by numerous groups who settled and took control of different areas. These groups included the Anglo-Saxons who were made up of the Angles, Saxons and Jutes arriving from Germany, Denmark and Holland.

Later on Britain was invaded by Viking groups from Scandinavia during the 9th century CE. Both the Anglo-Saxons and the Vikings had a lasting impact on the country.

In 1066, the Normans invaded England and successfully won at the Battle of Hastings. The Norman leader, William the Conqueror, successfully took over England and became king. The battle is portrayed in the Bayeux Tapestry, which is a very famous primary source that retells the entire battle through pictures along a tapestry that is about 70 metres in length!

■ **Figure 3.9** Section of the Bayeux Tapestry

■ **Figure 3.8** A helmet found at Sutton Hoo in England, the site of two Anglo-Saxon burial grounds

DISCUSS

What information does the source in Figure 3.9 provide about the Battle of Hastings and other battles at this time?

The tapestry was made on the orders of William's half-brother Odo. What do you think was the purpose of creating the Bayeux Tapestry?

EXTENSION

You can find out more about the Bayeux Tapestry by looking at this animation:

https://youtu.be/LtGoBZ4D4_E

LIFE IN ENGLAND

Life in England was mostly agricultural during the Middle Ages. Transport was slow, and most people walked or travelled on horseback. Despite the building of a network of roads during Roman times, the roads were not of a good quality. They would often get waterlogged and full of mud during bad weather and it was a very slow means of getting anywhere. In contrast, boats were a better means of transport during the Middle Ages which meant that ports developed as towns and small cities. Ports were also centres of trade with different parts of Europe.

Given this lack of mobility, people's lives were very much identified by the local area in which they lived. Most people lived in villages with farming being the dominant type of work.

The lord was typically the most important member of the village community, owning the land, collecting taxes and overseeing a system of law and order. The lords of the different areas of England tended to live in manor houses or castles, in stark contrast to the basic dwellings where the majority of people lived.

There were often punishments for people who did not pay their taxes or who broke the law. These punishments were often harsh and often involved some form of physical torture or humiliation. Some of the punishments seem barbaric and bizarre nowadays. A system called **'trial by ordeal'** was used to determine whether people were innocent of a particular crime. For example, trial by fire involved the accused walking over red-hot bars for a certain distance. If the wounds healed quickly the accused was said to be innocent. Over time, law courts were used instead of these ordeals.

Women often played a subservient role to men during the Middle Ages and had few rights. They were not able to choose their husband and often had to work hard in farming as well as bringing up children.

Religion played an important role in the daily life of people and the Catholic Church was influential in England during the Middle Ages. Numerous churches, abbeys and cathedrals were built as places of worship. Pilgrimage was an important tradition for many who could travel, and Canterbury in Kent in the south of England became an important pilgrimage site during this time.

■ **Figure 3.10** Commemorative stamps celebrating the 900th anniversary of the Domesday Book

THE DOMESDAY BOOK

After the Norman invasion of England, the new King William I wanted to get a better idea of the land he now controlled so he issued a survey to find out the population, land use and wealth of the villages across the land. This survey was compiled into the Domesday Book, which has proven to be an extremely useful source to historians studying England during this time. The Domesday Book is an example of a census used to measure the make-up of a country.

Chatham in Kent
Robert Latimer from Bishop of Bayeux, church, mill, 6 fisheries

Dartford in Kent
King's land, mill, 3 churches, 2 harbours

Wye in Kent
Battle Abbey, church, 4 mills, 300 eels

■ **Figure 3.11** Extracts from the Domesday Book from the county of Kent in the south of England

ACTIVITY: The Domesday Book

■ **ATL**

- Creative-thinking skills – Use brainstorming and visual diagrams to generate new ideas and inquiries; Create original works and ideas; use existing works and ideas in new ways

Figure 3.10 shows some commemorative stamps that were made in Britain in 1986 to celebrate the 900th anniversary of the Domesday Book.

1 **In groups**, look at each of the different scenes on the stamps in turn. Make a **list** of the different things that the stamps tell you about life in the Middle Ages. Write down any new questions that you have after looking at the pictures.
2 **Using** these pictures as inspiration and the information that you have looked at so far, write a piece of creative writing about life in England during the Middle Ages. Make sure you include different perspectives to highlight the different sections of society from the time, for example the differences between richer and poorer people.

◆ Assessment opportunities

This activity can be assessed using Criterion C: Communicating (strands i and ii) and Criterion D (strand iv).

Individuals and Societies for the IB MYP 2: *by Concept*

THE BLACK DEATH

Life in the Middle Ages was tough and the majority of people lived in pretty basic conditions. Life expectancy was short and many children died in the first year of their life.

Conditions got worse in times of war or during outbreaks of disease. During the 14th century, a particularly nasty disease known as the **Black Death** struck England, as well as many other parts of the world, causing a huge amount of suffering. The Black Death was the name given to the outbreak of bubonic plague at this time. Outbreaks of the plague had occurred throughout history but those in the 14th century were particularly severe.

The symptoms included fever, headaches and the growth of large buboes in areas such as the armpits and groin. The disease had a high mortality rate and people who contracted the disease could be dead within a couple of days. Rats carried the disease, then fleas that bit infected rats would pass the disease on to humans. At the time people did not know what caused the disease and often thought that it was a punishment from God.

It is thought that the disease initially started in Central Asia and travelled across to Europe due to the exchanges people made along the **Silk Road** that stretched across continental Asia and Europe. An outbreak was recorded in the Italian port city of Genoa in 1347, where it is believed that the disease arrived on boats from merchants who had travelled from the Black Sea. It is estimated that the Black Death killed approximately 40–60% of Europe's total population.

> ### DISCUSS
> What does the severity of the Black Death tell us about the medical knowledge and treatments available to people during the Middle Ages?
>
> Do some research online to find out what people at the time thought caused and would cure the disease.

> ### THINK–PAIR–SHARE
> Study Sources A and B on page 68.
>
> In pairs, **discuss** what each of the sources tells you about the Black Death and its impact.
>
> Share your thoughts with the rest of the class.

▼ Links to: Language and literature

Beowulf and The Canterbury Tales

Inquiries into historical time periods can be enriched by studying the literature from the time. *Beowulf* and *The Canterbury Tales* are two examples of literature from the Middle Ages in Europe.

Beowulf is an epic poem written some time during the early Middle Ages and set in Scandinavia. The poem tells the story of the warrior Beowulf who travels to an area where the Danes live to fight a monster called Grendel who has been terrorising the local population. In the story he has a number of battles against Grendel and other monsters and is eventually crowned as king. The story was very popular and provides an insight into some of the storytelling and folklore of the early Middle Ages in Europe.

The Canterbury Tales were written by Geoffrey Chaucer a lot later on in the Middle Ages, during the 14th century. *The Canterbury Tales* is a collection of stories that provide an insight into the structure of society in England towards the end of the Middle Ages. Stories include The Knight's Tale, The Cook's Tale and The Merchant's Tale.

■ Figure 3.12 Beowulf battling Grendel

■ Figure 3.13 Illustration from *The Canterbury Tales*

SOURCE A

Historia Roffensis by William Dene, a monk at Rochester Cathedral in Kent (in The Black Death *by Rosemary Horrox)*

A great mortality of men began in India. It raged through the whole of Egypt and Syria, and also through Greece, Italy and France, and came to England, where it destroyed more than a third of the men, women and children. Alas, this mortality killed so many that no one could be found to carry the bodies of the dead to burial, but men and women carried the bodies of their own little ones to church on their shoulders and threw them into mass graves, from which came such a stink that it was barely possible for anyone to go past a churchyard.

Such a shortage of workers followed that churchmen, knights and other great men were forced to thresh their corn, plough their own land and make their own bread. The shortage of workers in every kind of craft and job was so bad that more than a third of the land throughout the whole kingdom was left unfarmed.

SOURCE B

Chronicle of Geoffrey le Baker

People who one day had been full of happiness, on the next were found dead. Some were tormented by boils which broke out suddenly in various parts of the body, and were so hard and dry that when they were lanced hardly any liquid came out. Many of these people lived, by lancing the boils or by long suffering. Other victims had little black pustules scattered over their whole body. Of these, very few got better. The pestilence raged for more than a year in England and completely emptied many villages of human beings.

REFLECTION

How can works of literature provide us with a sense of a particular time period? Can you think of other examples of literature from other eras of history?

Which empires expanded their influence during the Middle Ages?

THE GOLDEN AGE OF ISLAM

The influence of Islam as a religion did not create a single unified empire, but it did unite several countries during the Middle Ages following the death of the Prophet Muhammad in 632CE. The religion spread its influence across the whole of Arabia and into areas of Africa, Asia and Europe after this time. Given the increased influence of the religion and the accompanying developments in the sciences, arts, trade and technology, the Middle Ages are often regarded as the Golden Age of Islam.

One location that was at the centre of many of these developments was the city of Baghdad. Baghdad became a centre of learning, as seen in the creation of the House of Wisdom. The House of Wisdom was the place where many of the great minds of the time met to collaborate on new ideas and inventions. Many works from the classical era were translated into Arabic. Christian and Jewish scholars also worked there. The city itself was also a showpiece of the best engineering at the time, with advanced systems of sanitation, and innovations that enhanced people's living standards, such as an abundance of parks.

A famous book written during this Golden Age was the *Book of Knowledge of Ingenious Mechanical Devices*, which detailed over 100 mechanical devices that could be constructed, including the Elephant Clock (Figure 3.14).

SOURCE A

Extract describing the city of Baghdad during the Golden Age of Islam

The city of Baghdad formed two vast semi-circles on the right and left banks of the Tigris, twelve miles in diameter. The numerous suburbs, covered with parks, gardens, villas and beautiful promenades, and plentifully supplied with rich bazaars, and finely built mosques and baths, stretched for a considerable distance on both sides of the river. In the days of its prosperity the population of Baghdad and its suburbs amounted to over two millions! The palace of the Caliph stood in the midst of a vast park several hours in circumference which beside a menagerie and aviary comprised an inclosure for wild animals reserved for the chase. The palace grounds were laid out with gardens, and adorned with exquisite taste with plants, flowers, and trees, reservoirs and fountains, surrounded by sculptured figures. On this side of the river stood the palaces of the great nobles. Immense streets, none less than forty cubits wide, traversed the city from one end to the other, dividing it into blocks or quarters, each under the control of an overseer or supervisor, who looked after the cleanliness, sanitation and the comfort of the inhabitants.

The water exits both on the north and the south were like the city gates, guarded night and day by relays of soldiers stationed on the watch towers on both sides of the river. Every household was plentifully supplied with water at all seasons by the numerous aqueducts which intersected the town; and the streets, gardens and parks were regularly swept and watered, and no refuse was allowed to remain within the walls.

https://legacy.fordham.edu/halsall/source/1000baghdad.asp

> ### DISCUSS
> According to Source A, why was Baghdad such an advanced city during the Middle Ages?

■ **Figure 3.14** The original design of the Elephant Clock in the *Book of Knowledge of Ingenious Mechanical Devices*

THE CRUSADES

The success of this Golden Age was put under pressure by a number of conflicts that occurred during the Middle Ages, which were known as The Crusades. The early Crusades mainly centred around capturing the city of Jerusalem. Jerusalem is a very important city for Christian, Jewish and Muslim people. During the 11th century, European Christians, upon the orders of Pope Urban II, successfully captured Jerusalem. This was the First Crusade. Perspectives on the significance of the Crusades vary.

The Crusades continued through the Middle Ages. Famous leaders on opposing sides include Richard the Lionheart, the King of England from 1189 to 1199, who was a noted military leader during the Third Crusade, and Saladin who was the first Sultan of the Ayyubid Dynasty who recaptured Jerusalem in 1187.

A positive consequence of the Crusades was the exchange of knowledge between different parts of

> **REFLECTION**
>
> What can the Golden Age of Islam teach us about the Middle Ages? Is it similar to or different from your initial ideas of the Middle Ages in the opening activity of the chapter?

the world. At the time the Islamic empire was more advanced than Europeans and the invading Europeans were able to gain knowledge of Islamic medicine and science, food and spices for cooking, castle design and gunpowder that had all been part of the results of the Golden Age. More significantly, the Mongol invasions of the 13th century placed greater pressure on the Islamic empire, with the sack of Baghdad and the destruction of the House of Wisdom, symbolising for many the end of this era.

■ **Figure 3.15** A modern reconstruction of the clock in a mall in Dubai

■ **Figure 3.16** Krak des Chevaliers, Syria – a Crusaders' castle

THE MONGOL EMPIRE

Spreading from their territory in Asia, the Mongol became the largest empire in the world during the Middle Ages and the largest land-based empire in history. The expansion of the Mongol empire mainly occurred due to the leadership of Genghis Khan. The Mongol people took over vast territories and ended the rule of a number of empires including the Kievan Rus in Europe and the Song Dynasty in China.

Traditionally the Mongols were **nomadic** herders who originated from the steppe areas of Mongolia. They were a tribal people who in many ways were an unlikely group to wield such influence, as they were often in conflict with each other. Genghis Khan was able to appeal to the mass population of Mongol people by killing and weakening the positions of richer people in Mongol society. His expansionism relied on the natural strengths of Mongol people on horseback and their skills in archery. At this time there were few rivals for global dominance and the Mongol empire was able to spread throughout continental Asia and into Arabia and Europe.

Mongol people are considered to have been quite bloodthirsty and many of their conquests involved large-scale murders. However, the Mongol expansion did not just bring about terror as they were able to rejuvenate important trade routes across the continent. For instance, the ancient silk route came back into prominence under the Mongol empire which promoted trade and exchange between different cultures. This was achieved by the establishment of the Pax Mongolica which brought peace to this trading route. Mongol people were also noted for their tolerance of different religious practices and more equitable status of women within society.

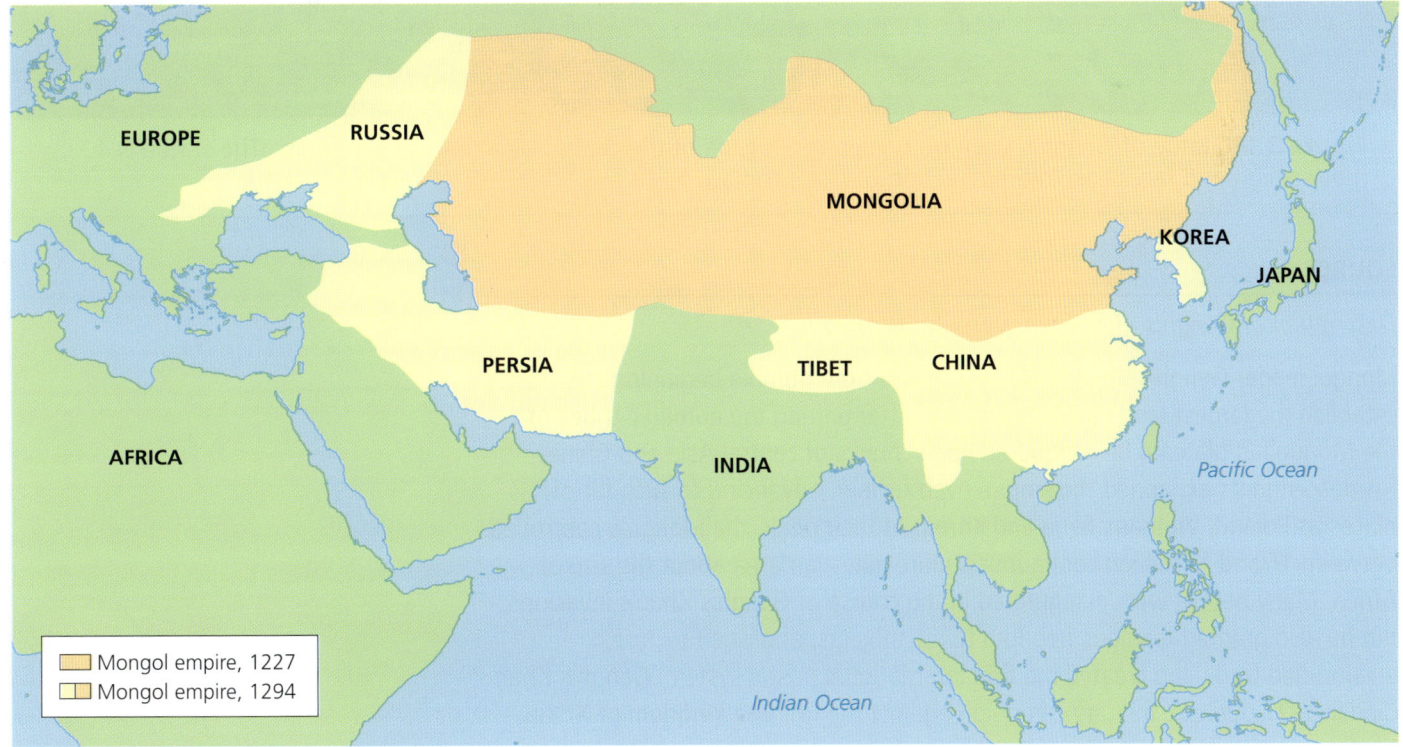

■ Figure 3.17 Map of the Mongol empire

SOURCE A

■ **Figure 3.18** Statue of Genghis Khan on horseback outside of the capital Ulaanbataar, Mongolia. The statue is 40 metres high and faces east in the direction of his birthplace

SOURCE B

Description of Genghis Khan from **www.history.com**

Mongol leader Genghis Khan (1162–1227) rose from humble beginnings to establish the largest land empire in history. After uniting the nomadic tribes of the Mongolian plateau, he conquered huge chunks of central Asia and China. His descendants expanded the empire even further, advancing to such far-off places as Poland, Vietnam, Syria and Korea. At their peak, the Mongols controlled between 11 and 12 million contiguous square miles, an area about the size of Africa. Many people were slaughtered in the course of Genghis Khan's invasions, but he also granted religious freedom to his subjects, abolished torture, encouraged trade and created the first international postal system. Genghis Khan died in 1227 during a military campaign against the Chinese kingdom of Xi Xia. His final resting place remains unknown.

SOURCE C

Source extracts from The Secret History of the Mongols *written during the 13th century. It is the oldest surviving work of literature about Genghis Khan and the Mongolian people*

Extract 1

Chingis* Khan took his army to Alashai and fought Asha Gambu.

They overcame the Tanghut forces on the plains there.

Asha Gambu retreated to a fort in the mountains of Alashai

but he was captured there and his people were defeated.

All his tents and all the wealth stored on the backs of his camels were taken,

and all his soldiers were killed,

blown away like the ashes of a fire gone out.

Chingis Khan ordered this, saying:

'Let our soldiers kill every Tanghut they can lay hands on,

let them slaughter any Tanghut soldier they can get.

Kill the bold and the brave ones,

put every capable Tanghut man to death.'

* Chinghis = Genghis

Extract 2

Once he had conquered the Moslem* people

Chingis Khan appointed agents to govern in each of their cities.

From the city of Gurganj came two Khwarezm Moslems,

a father and son named Yalavech and Masgud,

who explained to Chingis Khan the customs and laws of these cities

and the customs by which they were governed.

Chingis Khan appointed the Khwarezm Masgud head of the agents

who governed the cities of the Turkestan:

Bukhara, Samarkand, Gurganj, Khotan, Kashgar, Yarkand, and Kusen Tarim.

And his father Yalavech he made governor of the city of Chung-tu in Cathay.

Since among all the Moslems Yalavech and Masgud

were the most skilled at the customs and laws for governing cities,

he appointed them the governors of Cathay

along with our own agents.

* Moslem = Muslim

SOURCE D

A Daoist Sage, Changchun, visited and travelled with Genghis Khan. His writings are translated by Arthur Waley in The Travels of an Alchemist

At this season a fine rain begins to fall and the grass becomes green again. Then, after the middle of the eleventh month, the rain becomes heavier, sometimes turning to snow, and the ground becomes saturated. From the time of the Master's* first arrival in Samarkand it was his habit to give what grain we could spare to the poor and hungry of the city. Often, too, he would send hot rice-meal, and in this way saved a great number of lives.

* The reference to 'Master' is Genghis Khan.

ACTIVITY: Evaluating Genghis Khan

ATL

Critical-thinking skills – Evaluate evidence and arguments

1. Study Source A. What does the picture suggest about the importance of Genghis Khan to the people of Mongolia?
2. Copy and complete the following table.
3. **Using** the sources and any further research, **evaluate** the leadership of Genghis Khan. Aim to write approximately 500 words.

◆ Assessment opportunities

In this activity you have practised skills that are assessed using Criterion C: Communicating (strand ii) and Criterion D: Thinking critically (strand ii).

Source	What does it tell us about Genghis Khan?	Positive interpretations?	Negative interpretations?
A Photograph of a statue of Genghis Khan			
B Description of Genghis Khan from a popular history website			
C Extract 1 from *The Secret History of the Mongols*			
C Extract 2 from *The Secret History of the Mongols*			
D Extract from *The Travels of an Alchemist*			

Individuals and Societies for the IB MYP 2: *by Concept*

What was life like in China during the Middle Ages?

Imperial China dates back to the 3rd century BCE when the first emperor Qin ruled over China. He is famous for beginning the construction of the Great Wall of China and the burying of the terracotta warriors in and around his tomb.

Imperial China lasted from this time up until the beginning of the 20th century. During the Middle Ages there were a number of dynasties that ruled over China, though their territories varied depending on their military strength. One example of these dynasties was the Song Dynasty that ruled China between 960 and 1279CE.

Under these dynasties, China was known as the **Middle Kingdom**, and China very much viewed itself as the centre of the world. Much of the political structure of China during this time was influenced by the philosopher Confucius. Confucius lived in China during the 5th and 6th centuries BCE and proposed a number of ways that society should be ordered. He placed a great emphasis on harmony, family and respect for elders in society.

> By three methods we may learn wisdom: First, by reflection, which is noblest; Second, by imitation, which is easiest; and third by experience, which is the bitterest.

> The man who moves a mountain begins by carrying away small stones.

Figure 3.19 Statue of Confucius

> **DISCUSS**
>
> Read the quotations by Confucius. What do you think he meant?

THE SONG DYNASTY

Although conquered by Mongolia in the 13th century, the Song Dynasty represented a high point in Chinese history. Economically the developments during the era were significant in the areas of printing, agriculture and metal work.

The Song Dynasty was also the first to utilise gunpowder in conflict. A range of innovations demonstrate that this was an advanced society during the Middle Ages.

Despite these innovations there were major differences between the lives of Chinese people in cities compared with those in rural areas. People in rural areas typically lived in poverty, relying on farming as a way of life. Landowners had control in these areas. In the cities there was more wealth with people living increasingly sophisticated lives as seen in the developments in the arts and culture at the time.

■ **Figure 3.20** Liaodi Pagoda, constructed during the Song Dynasty

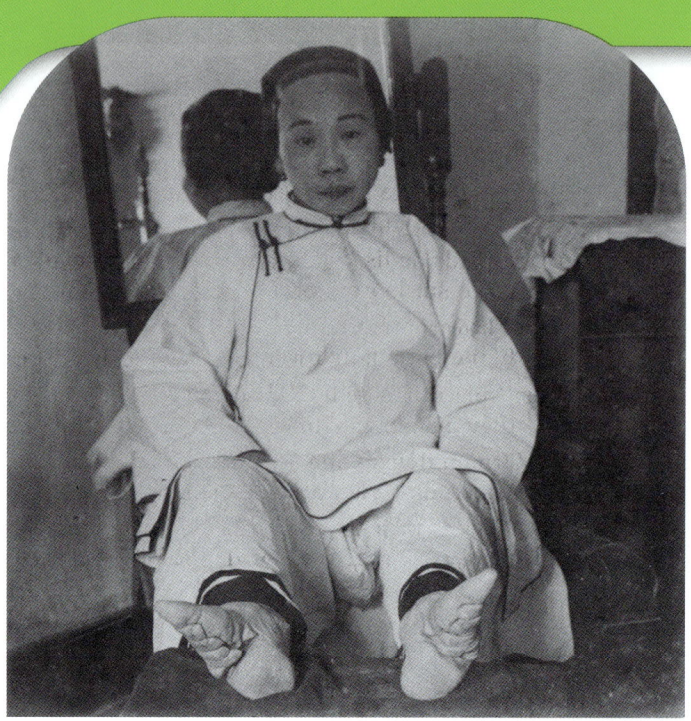

■ **Figure 3.21** Chinese woman with bound feet in the early 20th century

Innovation	Uses
Gunpowder	Fireworks and, later on, in conflict
Paper money	As currency
Compass	To determine magnetic north and for navigation
Movable type printing	To speed up the process of printing
Pagodas and bridges	In architecture – pagodas were often used for religious purposes
Canal system – locks	To develop the systems of canals – locks allowed water to move up and down so canals could link areas of different heights

■ **Table 3.1** Innovations of the Song Dynasty

Many traditions were established during the Song Dynasty, including **foot binding** for women. This was an extremely painful process which involved the reshaping of the foot by binding it into a pointed position so that the bones changed shape. Chinese women of upper-class backgrounds were often expected to have their feet bound to demonstrate to others their wealth, but for many this led to a life of disability and severely restricted movement.

DISCUSS

What effect do you think the practice of foot binding would have had on the lives of women in China?

ACTIVITY: What was life like in the Middle Ages?

■ ATL

- Critical-thinking skills – Gather and organize relevant information to formulate an argument
- Communication skills – Organize and depict information logically

For this task you need to choose a location on which to focus and then **explore** some of the different features of life in that area during the Middle Ages.

You can choose one of the examples from this chapter or pick a different location that has not been covered. The Middle Ages is a big topic spanning a large amount of time so we really have only scratched the surface in this chapter! Here are some options you could look at:

- The Byzantine empire
- Kingdom of Franks
- Kievan Rus
- The Mongol Empire
- The Song Dynasty in China
- Medieval Britain
- The Axum empire in Africa

Try to answer these questions within your project:
- When were they around?
- What factors led to their establishment?
- Where were they based? (You could include a map here.)
- What were some of their achievements?
- What would it have been like to live there?
- What was life like for women?
- Why did they come to an end?

Try to bring in different perspectives to give your work more depth. Locating primary and secondary sources will help you with your research on this task.

For Criterion B you will need to construct an action plan to help you with the **investigation**. The action plan should detail your organization and time frame for the task. It should also detail your research as you gather evidence to place in your project. When you have finished, you should complete an **evaluation** to reflect on the research, process and results of your project. The table below can be used as a guide to help you to complete this evaluation.

◆ Assessment opportunities

In this activity you have practised skills that are assessed using Criterion A (strands i and ii), Criterion B (strands ii, iii and iv) and Criterion C: Communicating (strands i, ii and iii).

Stage	What went well?	What didn't go as planned?	What could you do differently next time?
Research (gathering information, taking notes, keeping a record of your references)			
Process (writing the project, time keeping, organizing the information and the structure)			
Results (the finished product, overall quality of the project in terms of writing, presentation)			

Research skills

Before you go straight to the internet to research this task, remember to consider the different resources at your disposal, including your school or local library! You would be surprised at the wealth of information you can find by going to the library. Books, encyclopedias, journals and magazines can really help you with these types of tasks as well as good quality websites. When researching, always remember to think carefully about what you would like to find. Good luck researching!

! Take action

- ! National History Day is an organization that encourages students around the world to conduct historical research and investigation. Have a look at their website to see if there are any opportunities for you to take action and do some first-hand research into historical topics that are of interest to you: www.nhd.org

DISCUSS

Has the Middle Ages been misrepresented in history?

What do you think? How would you describe the Middle Ages from what you have learned in this chapter? Do you think it was a difficult time for people or a time of progress? **Discuss** your ideas in groups to reflect upon your learning.

Reflection

In this chapter, we have seen that the Middle Ages was a time when there were many challenges facing people, such as conflict, disease and inequality. Despite these issues, we have seen examples of progress in science, technology and systems of law that gradually helped societies to develop. As a period of history it is vast and there is much more that can be looked at and explored to gain insights into the lives of people during this time.

Use this table to reflect on your own learning in this chapter.					
Questions we asked	Answers we found	Any further questions now?			
Factual: When was the Middle Ages? What was the impact of the decline of the Roman empire? How was society structured during the Middle Ages? What was life like in Britain during the Middle Ages? Which empires expanded their influence during the Middle Ages? What was life like in China during the Middle Ages?					
Conceptual: What perspectives can be used to study the past? Why is continuity important to the study of history?					
Debatable: Has the Middle Ages been misrepresented in history?					
Approaches to learning you used in this chapter	Description – what new skills did you learn?	How well did you master the skills?			
		Novice	Learner	Practitioner	Expert
Communication skills					
Critical-thinking skills					
Creative-thinking skills					
Learner profile attribute(s)	Reflect on the importance of being knowledgeable for your learning in this chapter.				
Knowledgeable					

Global interactions | Causality | Orientation in space and time

4 How does exploration affect global interactions?

In the past, humans explored the world, and continue to do so, for a variety of reasons. This exploration often affects global interactions in both positive and negative ways.

CONSIDER THESE QUESTIONS:

Factual: How did exploration affect early societies? What were the causes and consequences of the 'Age of Exploration'? How did industrialization affect exploration? What examples are there of female explorers? What examples are there of exploration in the 21st century?

Conceptual: Why do people explore? What are the causes and consequences of exploration?

Debatable: Does exploration lead to exploitation?

Now **share and compare** your thoughts and ideas with your partner, or with the whole class.

■ Figure 4.1 Mountaineers and travellers

IN THIS CHAPTER, WE WILL …

- **Find out** about exploration at different times in history as well as its importance in the 21st century.
- **Explore** the reasons why people explore and the different consequences of exploration.
- **Take action** by considering the ways that exploration can bring positive consequences to people's lives.

80 Individuals and Societies for the IB MYP 2: *by Concept*

- ■ These Approaches to Learning (ATL) skills will be useful …
  - Communication skills
  - Information literacy skills
  - Critical-thinking skills

- ● We will reflect on this learner profile attribute …
  - **Risk-takers** – as exploration nearly always involves some kind of risk.

- ◆ Assessment opportunities in this chapter:
  - ◆ **Criterion A**: Knowing and understanding
  - ◆ **Criterion B**: Investigating
  - ◆ **Criterion C**: Communicating
  - ◆ **Criterion D**: Thinking critically

ACTIVITY: 3, 2, 1 bridge

Individually, on sticky notes or paper, write down:

3 thoughts and ideas

2 questions

1 analogy

… about the word 'exploration'.

Once you have finished, share your ideas with other members of the class. At the end of the chapter, repeat the activity to find out what similarities and differences there are as a result of the inquiry in this chapter.

KEY WORDS

conquest	explore
industrialization	navigation
empire	missionaries

4 How does exploration affect global interactions?

Why do people explore?

WHAT IS EXPLORATION?

Exploration is defined as a process of discovery, seeking out new ways of looking at things. Throughout history, there have been many examples of people exploring the world for different reasons. People have explored the world to find resources, to set up trade with other civilizations, to conquer and control and as a form of adventure. In this chapter, we will inquire into different historical and contemporary examples of exploration to gain an understanding of its causes, consequences and how it affects the world.

Cargoes

Quinquireme of Nineveh from distant Ophir,
Rowing home to haven in sunny Palestine,
With a cargo of ivory,
And apes and peacocks,
Sandalwood, cedarwood, and sweet white wine.

Stately Spanish galleon coming from the Isthmus,
Dipping through the Tropics by the palm-green shores,
With a cargo of diamonds,
Emeralds, amethysts,
Topazes, and cinnamon, and gold moidores.

Dirty British coaster with a salt-caked smoke stack,
Butting through the Channel in the mad March days,
With a cargo of Tyne coal,
Road-rails, pig-lead,
Firewood, iron-ware, and cheap tin trays.

John Masefield

DISCUSS

What is the message of this poem? What is the connection with exploration?

■ Figure 4.2 Trade and exploration

Individuals and Societies for the IB MYP 2: *by Concept*

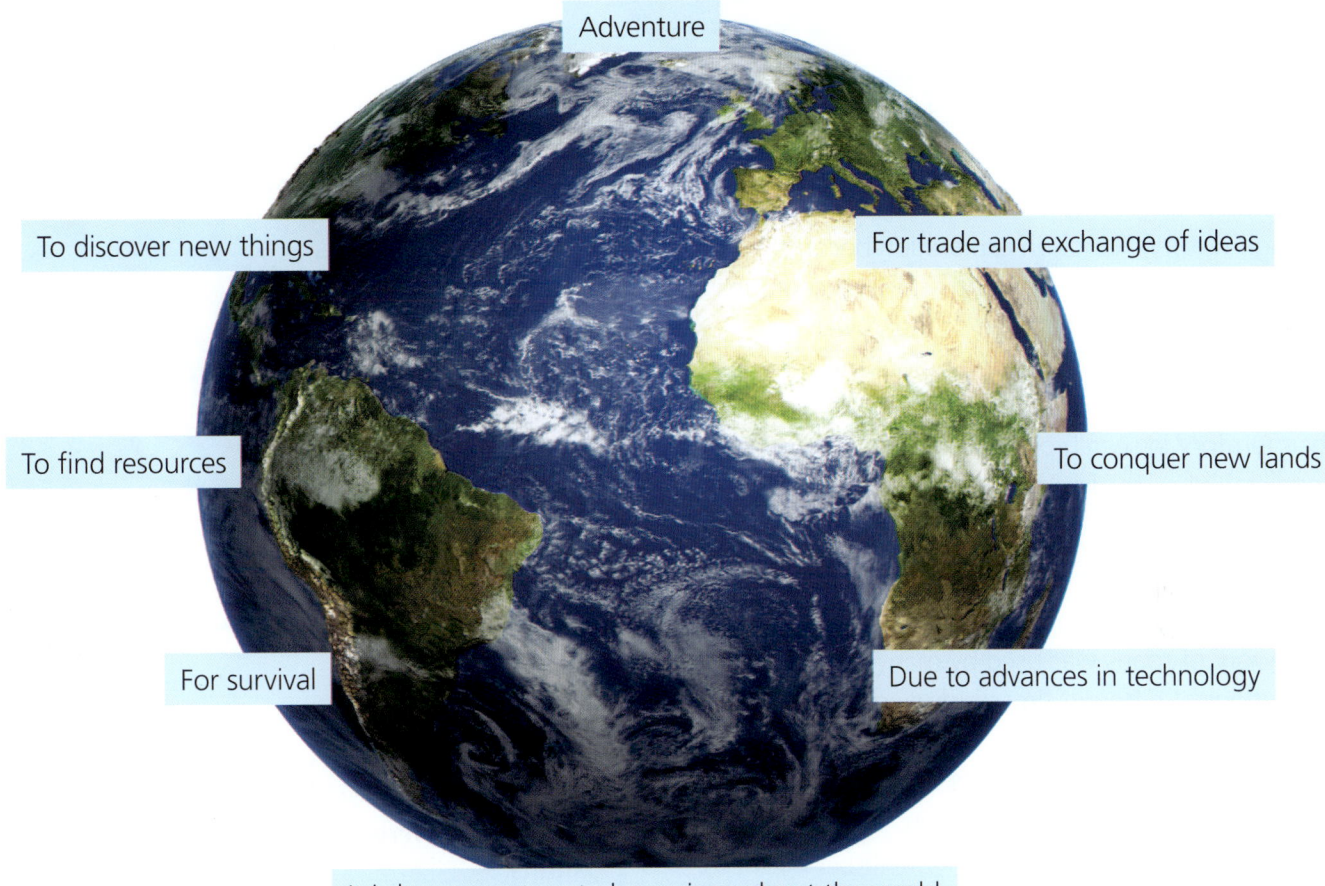

■ **Figure 4.3** Why do people explore?

ACTIVITY: Why do people explore?

■ ATL

Critical-thinking skills – Gather and organize relevant information to formulate an argument

1 Make a copy of the diagram in Figure 4.3 and add in ideas and examples in each of the boxes for why they are reasons for different types of human exploration. For example, for the 'advances in technology' box you could include the development of transport and how that would affect exploration.

2 In groups, categorise the reasons in order of importance. This could be done in a 'diamond nine' format. **Discuss** and debate the significance of each of the factors to build consensus or reflect on the differences between the members of the group.
3 Finally, in groups, choose one of the reasons to focus on in more detail. **Create** a short presentation based on your research. It should link to the question 'Why do people explore?' Aim for it to be approximately five minutes long.

◆ Assessment opportunities

This activity can be assessed using Criterion C: Communicating (strands i and ii).

How did exploration affect early societies?

Exploration has been a consistent theme running through history. Although exploration became a major global phenomenon in the 15th and 16th centuries during the Age of Exploration or the Voyages of Discovery, exploration occurred before this time. Many of the early civilizations of the world expanded their territory in search of new lands and resources, and established trading routes. This mostly occurred through land-based travel but a number of maritime routes also developed.

The Silk Road which linked Europe with Asia across a network of roads was used by many different civilizations at different times including the Chinese, Persian and Roman empires. The roads crossed difficult terrain including deserts such as the Gobi, as well as mountainous areas. Caravans that travelled the routes were at constant risk of being attacked by bandits. Despite the dangers, the Silk Road established important trading routes between different civilizations and also allowed for the exchange of ideas and culture.

■ **Figure 4.5** Caravan of travellers and camels in the desert

DISCUSS

Much of the Silk Road travel was carried out by groups of people with camels. They travelled in groups to transport cargo such as the silks or spices and were often subject to attacks by bandits.

What do you think were some of the challenges facing these travellers?

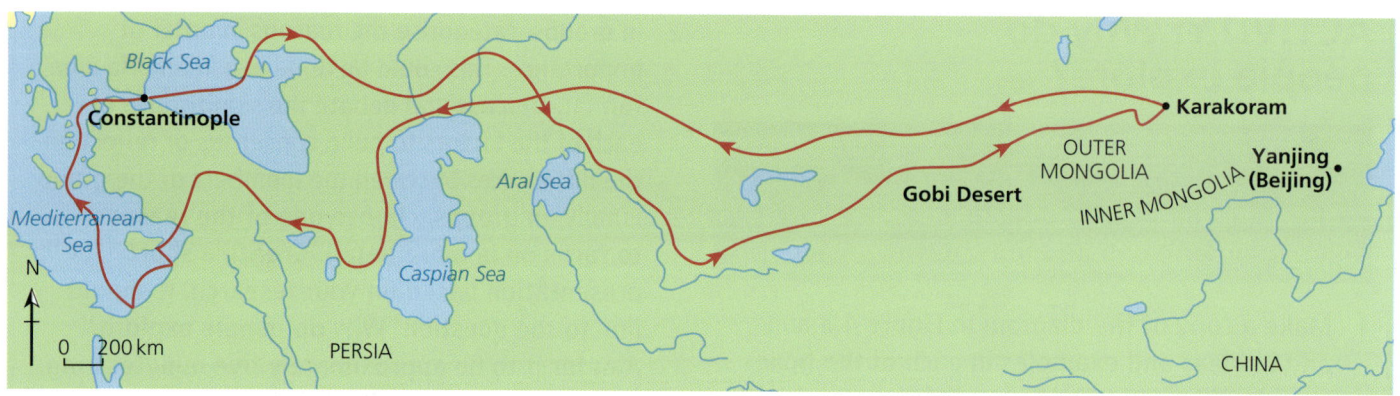

■ **Figure 4.4** Map of the Silk Road

MARCO POLO

A famous early explorer, Marco Polo wrote down his experiences of travel. He was a European merchant from Venice who travelled across continental Europe and Asia, including the silk roads, to reach Kublai Khan, the emperor of the Yuan Dynasty of Imperial China. Khan was a Mongol ruler who had established the Yuan Dynasty in China after defeating the Song Dynasty (see page 76).

Although Marco Polo was not the first European to reach China, his writings about his travels form an important record of early exploration. Polo travelled with his father and uncle for the journey across remote stretches of Asia before reaching China.

When they finally arrived, they ended up working for Kublai Khan for many years before making a perilous journey back to Venice that lasted two years. Three years after he returned to Venice, Marco Polo was placed in prison for a time for leading a battle against the rival city state of Genoa. In prison he wrote his *Book of Marvels of the World* or, more commonly, *The Travels of Marco Polo*. It has been widely read and has become an inspiration for other explorers and travellers ever since.

■ **Figure 4.6** Marco Polo

ACTIVITY: The Travels of Marco Polo

■ **ATL**

Critical-thinking skills – Draw reasonable conclusions and generalizations

Read Sources A and B, taken from *The Travels of Marco Polo*, and then answer the following questions.

1. What do the extracts tell us about the benefits and opportunities of Marco Polo's travels? What does he find out about?
2. What do the extracts tell us about the dangers of Marco Polo's travels? How does he overcome these dangers?
3. Complete a source **evaluation** of *The Travels of Marco Polo*. You can use the table to help you. Think about its values and limitations for finding out about exploration during the time. Why might it be useful to historians?

Origin	
Purpose	
Values	
Limitations	

◆ **Assessment opportunities**

This activity can be assessed using Criterion D: Thinking critically (strands ii and iii).

SOURCE A

From *The Travels of Marco Polo*, Chapter XIX 'The Descent To The City of Hormos'

The Plain of which we have spoken extends in a southerly direction for five days' journey, and then you come to another descent another twenty miles in length, where the road is very bad and full of peril, for there are many robbers and bad characters about. When you have got to the foot of this descent you find another beautiful plain called the Plain of Formosa. This extends for two days' journey; and then you find in it fine streams of water with plenty of date-palms and other fruit-trees. There are also many beautiful birds, francolins, popinjays and other kinds such as we have none of in our country. When you have ridden these two days you come to the Ocean Sea, and on the shore you find a city with a harbour which is called Hormos. Merchants come thither from India, with ships loaded with spidery and precious stones, pearls, cloths of silk and gold, elephants' teeth, and many other wares, which they sell to the merchants of Hormos, and which these in turn carry all over the world to dispose of again.

SOURCE B

From *The Travels of Marco Polo*, Chapter XX 'The Wearisome and Desert Road That Now Has To Be Traveled'

On departing from the city of Kerman you find the road for seven days most wearisome; and I will tell you how this is. The first three days you meet with no water, or next to none. And what little you do meet with is bitter green stuff, so salt that no one can drink it; and in fact if you drink a drop of it, it will set you purging ten times at least by the way … In all those three days you meet with no human habitation; it is all desert, and the extremity of drought. Even of wild beasts there are none, for there is nothing for them to eat. After those three days in the desert you arrive at a stream of fresh water running underground … It has an abundant supply, and travellers, worn from the hardships of the desert, here rest and refresh themselves and their beasts.

What were the causes and consequences of the 'Age of Exploration'?

Exploration became a global phenomenon during the 15th, 16th and 17th centuries. It was during this time that many European explorers navigated large areas of the world that had not previously been mapped or travelled to by Europeans. Portuguese and Spanish explorers in particular played an important role during this time. This occurred during a broader time period called the **Renaissance** (which we will look at in Chapter 6), a time of numerous developments in the sciences, arts and mathematics.

More adventurous types of exploration could take place during this time due to a number of developments. Improved technology made long-distance travel by sea more achievable. Advances in the fields of navigation and map making were particularly significant in allowing this to occur. A technique called 'dead reckoning' was used to navigate the seas, which involved mathematical processes to determine one's position based on a previous fixed point and the speed and course of the journey that had been taken.

Maritime exploration was organised in order to make profits by accessing new markets and resources. Many of the established trade routes (for example the older silk road) had been blocked by the spread of the Ottoman empire during this time. New trade routes around the world were therefore needed. Indian Ocean trade flourished during this time with various ports established on the East African and Indian coastlines.

In addition, Spanish and Portuguese exploration led to the discovery and colonization of the Americas. Large sections of the Americas were gradually taken over by these explorers.

> ▼ **Links to: Mathematics**
>
> Navigation requires an understanding of mathematics. Do some inquiry into some of the **mathematics of navigation**.
>
> Search for the **TED-Ed talk** on **'How does math guide our ships at sea?'** to learn more about this topic.

■ **Figure 4.7** The caravel was an example of the improvements in sailing boats during the Age of Exploration. Developed in Portugal, it was highly manoeuvrable and used for oceanic exploration

The following are some of the key figures and their significant achievements in the field of exploration during this time.

CHRISTOPHER COLUMBUS

Facts
Italian explorer from Genoa (1451–1506)

Achievements
Credited with the discovery of the Americas in 1492, leading on to European colonisation and the Columbian Exchange.

BARTOLEMEU DIAS

Facts
Portuguese explorer (1451–1500)

Achievements
Discovered the Cape of Good Hope off the coast of South Africa, which became a maritime route around the southern tip of Africa and into the Indian Ocean.

ZHENG HE

Facts
Chinese explorer during Ming Dynasty (1371–1433)

Achievements
Carried out multiple maritime journeys and brought back various goods to China, including animals native to Africa. Regarded as one of China's greatest explorers.

■ Figure 4.8 Explorers

VASCO DA GAMA

Facts
Portuguese explorer (lived from sometime in the 1460s until 1524)

Achievements
First European explorer to reach India by sea. This led to stronger trading connections between Asia and Europe and the further development of Indian Ocean trade.

FERDINAND MAGELLAN

Facts
Portuguese explorer who was an expert navigator (1480–1521)

Achievements
His expedition was the first to circumnavigate the world. Died in the Philippines during a conflict there in 1521.

SIR FRANCIS DRAKE

Facts
English explorer and politician (1540–96)

Achievements
Successfully circumnavigated the world. Also fought in the conflicts between Spain and England during this time.

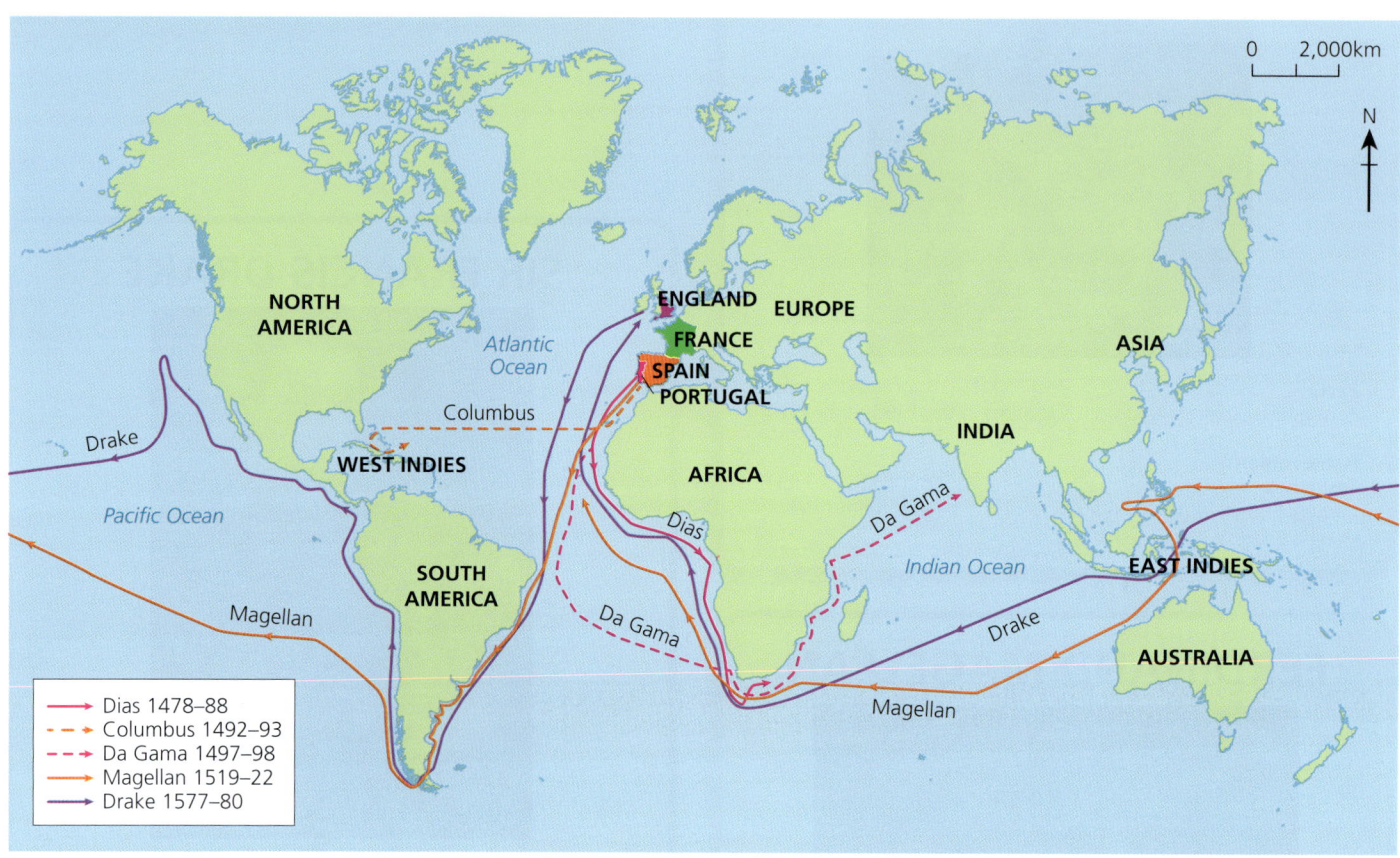

■ **Figure 4.9** Map showing some of the Voyages of Discovery

REFLECTION: Significant individuals

Inquiries into historical time periods often invite discussion of significant individuals who were said to have an impact on events and processes at the time. The importance of individuals to historical events is debatable and worth reflecting on in more detail.

- What significant individuals can you think of from history?
- What makes someone significant? Does it have to be a positive impact?
- What do you think are the values and limitations of studying significant individuals when exploring a historical time period?
- We have been looking at explorers in this chapter. Do you think there may be many other explorers from different time periods which we are not aware of? Why might this be the case?

ACTIVITY: Creating a biography

■ ATL

Communication skills – Write for different purposes

Choose one of the explorers detailed on pages 88–89 or someone from later on in the chapter (see pages 102–103). **Create** a short (one- or two-page) illustrated biography of the explorer to highlight their achievements. Remember to include a bibliography of the sources used when researching.

The following questions can be used to guide your writing:
- **What was their background?**
- **What were their main achievements (or failures) as explorers?**
- **What has been their significance?**

Include a map to show the route(s) they took in their exploration.

◆ Assessment opportunities

In this activity you have practised skills that are assessed using Criterion A: Knowing and understanding (strands i and ii), Criterion B: Investigating (strand iii) and Criterion C: Communicating (strands i, ii and iii).

> **DISCUSS**
>
> What do you think were the positive and negative consequences of the Columbian Exchange? Take a look at the map in Figure 4.10. In pairs, **discuss** the impact that the exchange of the different goods would have on people in the Old and New Worlds.

THE COLUMBIAN EXCHANGE

One significant consequence of the European discovery of the Americas was the widespread exchange of goods, ideas and culture between the Old World (Europe, Asia and Africa) and the New World (the Americas). This exchange has become known as the **Columbian Exchange** after the book written by the historian Alfred Crosby in 1972.

In his book, Crosby explains that the discovery of the Americas in 1492 had global significance because of the exchange of animals, plants, people and diseases that occurred. For example, a vast variety of foods were exchanged, including the potato, tomato and cacao going from the New to the Old World, and the apple, turnip and lettuce travelling in the other direction. This affected the diet of people around the world; the potato became a major staple of the European diet as a result.

Unfortunately, it also led to the spread of diseases. Diseases from the Old World had a devastating effect on many of the native populations of the Americas; these diseases included smallpox, the flu and typhus.

The exchange of animals was also significant. The horse, for example, was very beneficial to many Native North Americans who were able to use it to hunt more effectively. The Columbian Exchange can be viewed as an example of globalization due to its impact across the world, bringing lasting negative and positive consequences, and highlights the impact of exploration on the world.

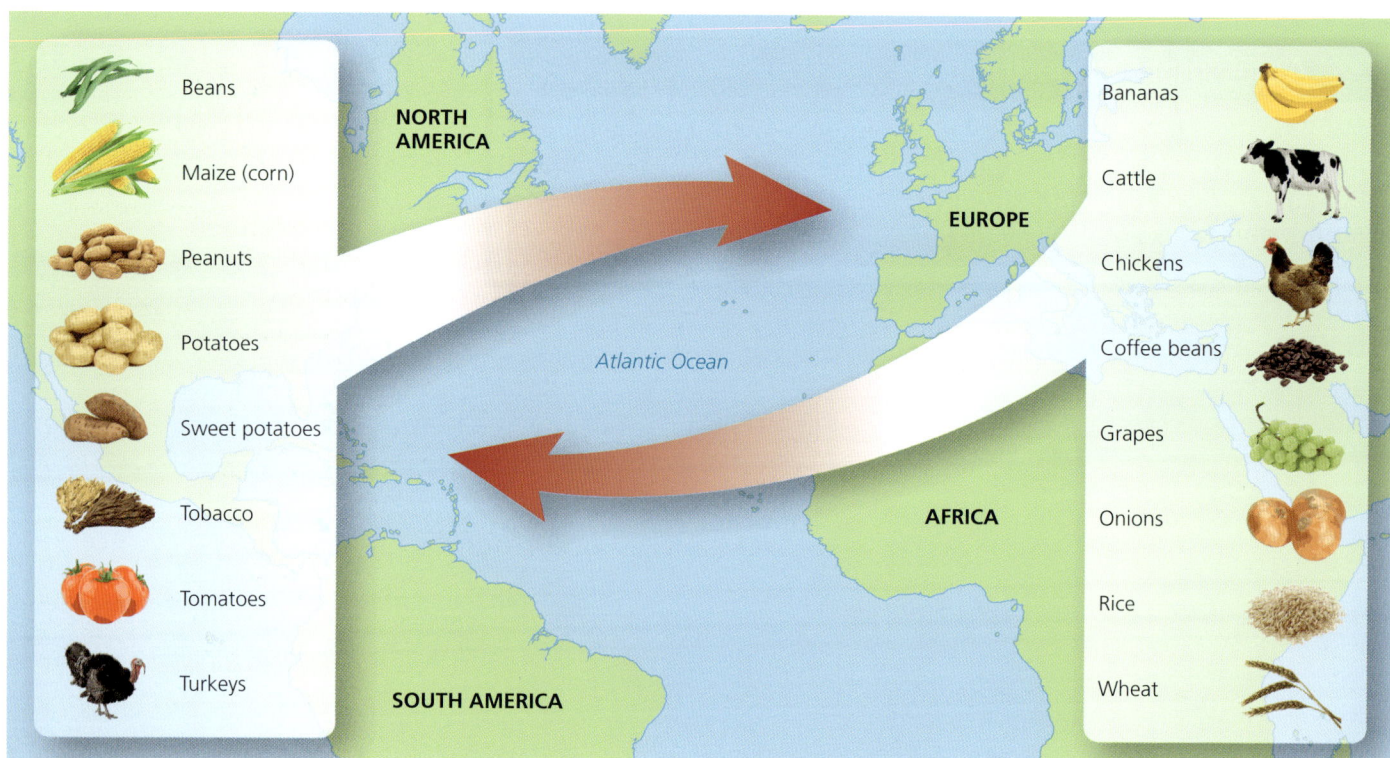

■ Figure 4.10 Examples of goods exchanged after 1492

WHO WERE THE CONQUISTADORS?

The Spanish and Portuguese explorers making in-roads to the Americas were known as 'conquistadors', which is translated as conquerors. These people were soldiers of their respective empires who were well trained in military affairs. They were often accompanied by religious figures of the Catholic Church who worked as missionaries. Missionaries are people who spread religion in different areas of the world. They played a significant role in the spread of the Catholic religion into South America during this time period. Famous conquistadors included Hernán Cortés, who conquered the Aztec empire, and Francisco Pizarro, who conquered the Inca empire.

The Spanish conquests of the Aztec and Inca empires led to the creation of the Vice Royalty of New Spain and the Vice Royalty of Peru in the 16th century. The Spanish administered these areas and also sought to find valuable resources. In particular, they were looking for gold and silver. Legends of a city of gold, El Dorado, added to the sense of adventure at this time. Although they did find some gold, they found much larger quantities of silver. Spanish colonists established mines to extract this precious metal. The native populations were used as cheap labour in dangerous working conditions, and the silver was shipped back to Spain and used as currency. However, high levels of inflation led to the devaluing of the silver over time.

The Spanish and Portuguese exploration of the Americas was a significant global event due to the impact of the Columbian Exchange and the development of many areas. However, the negative impact of disease and the subjugation of native civilizations such as Aztec and Inca mean that it can be viewed in a negative light.

Formulating research questions

Writing questions is harder than it sounds. You need to try to create a question with a clear focus. One thing that really helps when writing questions is using command terms. The following command terms from the *MYP Individuals and Societies Guide* could work well for this task:

- Analyse
- Explain
- Discuss
- Evaluate
- Explore

A good way to practise writing questions is to write a big list of questions that you think will allow you to discuss the impact of explorers on the world. Aim to write about 20 different questions. Then, with help from others or alone, start to discard the questions that you don't think would work well. Think about what makes a good question! It should be clear and focused and ideally use a command term.

For example:
- **How has exploration affected the world?** This would be too broad in scope to cover in 500–800 words.

Whereas:
- **Analyse the impact of two explorers on the world.** This would be more focused and appropriate for the task.
- **Discuss the achievements of Christopher Columbus and Vasco Da Gama.** This allows you to **discuss** and **compare** the two explorers' achievements

Remember that good questions should be focused and treatable in the number of words available for your assignment. Good luck!

SOURCE A

It was gold and silver that drove the Spanish on in their exploration and conquest of the Americas. By the 1530s, less than 50 years after Christopher Columbus had reached the New World, the Spanish had succeeded in conquering the two superpowers of the region, the Aztec and the Inca empires. Yet, the encounter with these powerful empires, and the material wealth gained from them served only to fire the imagination and increase the European lust for gold. Both before and after the destruction of these empires, legends about fabled cities and places filled with gold, silver and other precious objects arose amongst the conquistadors, sending the explorers ever deeper into the interior of the continent. One of the legends circulating amongst them was that of the Sierra de la Plata.

Sierra de la Plata literally means 'Mountain of Silver', and is a legend about a city that was filled with a quantity of silver that was almost inconceivable.

www.ancient-origins.net

SOURCE B

■ **Figure 4.11** Illustration of the Silver Mountain near the city of Potosi

SOURCE C

An extract from History Today *by Tim Stanley*

The Aztecs were unable to resist the Spanish partly due to technological and strategic inferiority, but mainly because their society was already on the brink of collapse. History shows that a civilization will only survive so long as it deserves to survive. A society that grows so decadent and violent that it can no longer function can become sterile and self-destructive. As went the Aztecs, so went the Athenians, the Romans, the Qing Dynasty, Nazi Germany and the Soviet Union. Most were overcome by force of arms, granted. But they had already begun to rot from within.

SOURCE D

Read the first three paragraphs of the section about the Columbian Exchange in this article about the conquistadors.

www.bbc.co.uk/history/british/tudors/conquistadors_01.shtml

ACTIVITY: The Spanish conquests of the Americas

ATL

Information literacy skills – Access information to be informed and to inform others

1. What do Sources A and B tell us about the motives of the conquistadors in their exploration of the Americas?
2. What point is the writer of Source C making?
3. What does Source D suggest about the consequences of the Columbian Exchange?
4. 'The Spanish conquests of the Americas negatively affected the world.' Do you agree? **Explain** your answer using the sources and your own knowledge.

Assessment opportunities

In this activity you have practised skills that are assessed using Criterion A: Knowing and understanding (strands i and ii) and Criterion D: Thinking critically (strands i and ii).

DISCUSS

Think about these questions: To what extent can we argue that the exploration of the world by European travellers was simply a self-serving exercise? Does exploration bring any benefits to those people who become colonized? You could think of a range of ideas and examples here and continue to reflect on these questions throughout the chapter.

How did industrialization affect exploration?

During the 19th century, the world continued to be explored and mapped by various people; this included the exploration of Africa and Oceania.

It was during this time that the industrial revolutions had reached a number of European countries including Britain and France; they reached the USA and Japan later on, in the 19th century. Industrialization led to developments in railways and shipping which made transport far quicker. For instance, the development of railways meant that people could increasingly travel across their country with relative ease. The invention of steam ships meant that large quantities of goods could be traded with different areas of the world, which increased the importance of port cities. Industrialization also meant that new products were being manufactured and subsequently traded around the world. Another invention, the telegraph, meant that messages could be communicated across the world over electrical lines in the form of Morse code, which was the precursor to the telephone.

■ Steam locomotive (1814)

■ Bicycle (1839)

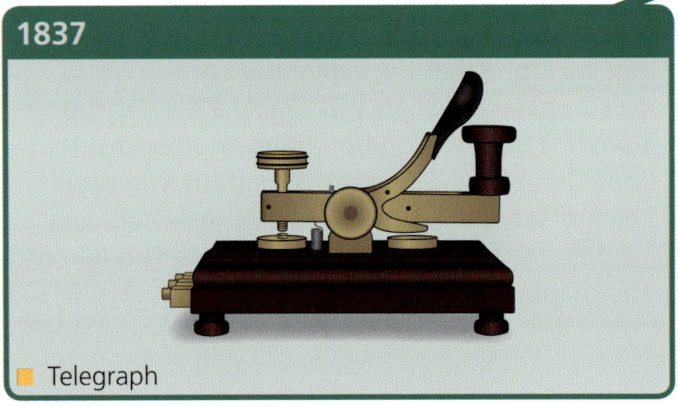
■ Telegraph (1837)

■ Telephone (1876)

■ **Figure 4.12** Timeline of industrialization

> **DISCUSS**
> Take a look at the inventions of the industrial revolutions in transport, communication and entertainment shown in Figure 4.12. How do you think each of them would affect exploration?

1885 Automobile

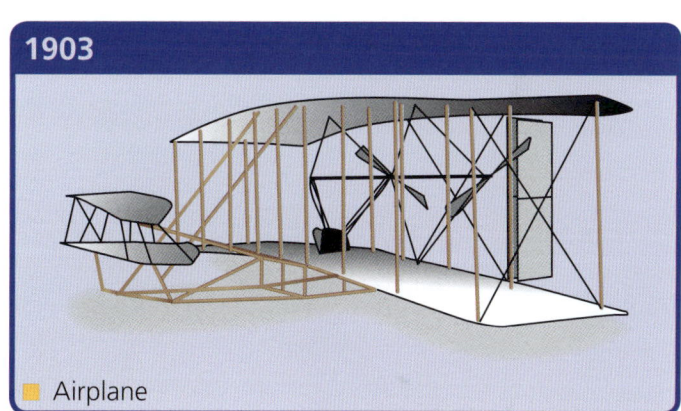
1903 Airplane

1865　1870　1875　1880　1885　1890　1895　1900　1905　1910

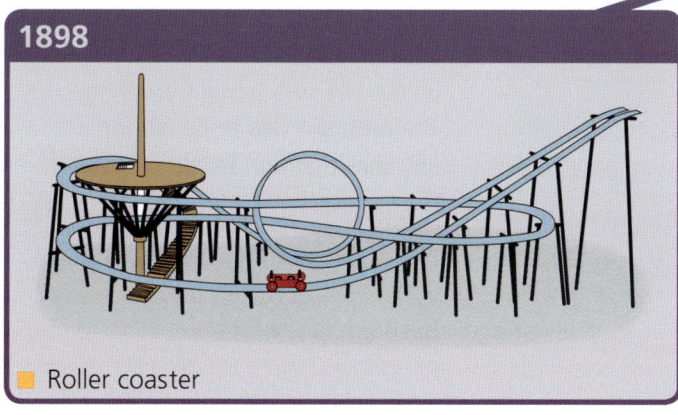
1898 Roller coaster

1908 Model T Ford

4   How does exploration affect global interactions?

THE EXPANSION OF EMPIRES

The 19th century saw the expansion of empires as the industrializing countries sought to expand their influence into other areas of the world. For example, by the end of the 19th century the African continent had been divided into colonies by different imperialist European countries. Driven in part by the process of exploration, a lot of empire building was about nationalism and economic considerations. Countries were looking to increase their influence and power around the world.

SOURCE A

■ **Figure 4.13** Africa under colonialism at the beginning of the 20th century

SOURCE B

Extract about the Berlin Conference of 1885

Representatives of 13 European states, the United States of America and the Ottoman empire converged on Berlin at the invitation of German Chancellor Otto von Bismarck to divide up Africa among themselves 'in accordance with international law.' Africans were not invited to the meeting.

The Berlin Conference led to a period of heightened colonial activity by the European powers. With the exception of Ethiopia and Liberia, all the states that make up present-day Africa were parcelled out among the colonial powers within a few years after the meeting. Lines of longitude and latitude, rivers and mountain ranges were pressed into service as borders separating the colonies. Or one simply placed a ruler on the map and drew a straight line. Many historians, such as Olyaemi Akinwumi from Nasarawa State University in Nigeria, see the conference as the crucible for future inner African conflicts.

'In African Studies, many of us believe that the foundation for present day crises in Africa was actually laid by the 1884/85 Berlin Conference. The partition was done without any consideration for the history of the society.'

www.dw.com/en/130-years-ago-carving-up-africa-in-berlin/a-18278894

98   Individuals and Societies for the IB MYP 2: *by Concept*

SOURCE C

■ **Figure 4.14** Political cartoon about the Berlin Conference

> **ACTIVITY: Exploration and the expansion of empires**
>
> ■ **ATL**
>
> Information literacy skills – Make connections between various sources of information
>
> 1 What does the map in Source A suggest about the extent of European influence in Africa by the beginning of the 20th century? What impact do you think colonization would have on the exploration of Africa?
> 2 What is the message of the cartoon in Source C?
> 3 According to Source B, what were some of the long-term consequences of the Berlin Conference? What does it tell us about the negative consequences of exploration?

THE GROWTH OF TOURISM AND GLOBETROTTING

Technological improvements also led to the development of a new type of exploration: tourism. This provided opportunities for individuals to travel much further than before, more quickly and more cheaply.

Developments in transport in the 19th century saw the establishment of tourist towns in many countries. These were often coastal towns that provided a holiday destination for the people who lived nearby. For example, Brighton on the south coast of England was able to attract far more visitors after the building of the direct railway line to London. Atlantic City in the USA developed as a coastal tourist town under a similar process.

Richer individuals were able to pursue their wanderlust for exploration during the 19th century as the new transport options meant that more travel could be done for leisure. Some of these individuals were referred to as '**globetrotters**'. A famous example was Rudyard Kipling, who spent a considerable amount of time in India, the USA, South Africa and Japan. He wrote *The Jungle Book* based on his time in India.

Another popular book from the time, by Jules Verne and published in 1873, is *Around the World in 80 Days*, in which the main character Phileas Fogg travels across the world in 80 days. Although a work of fiction, the book draws upon the technological developments of the era that made global travel a possibility and can be used to explore attitudes towards travel at that time. For instance, the building and opening of the Suez Canal made journeys for ships going from Europe to Asia significantly quicker as they no longer needed to travel around Africa. The book was also a source of inspiration for many who sought adventure and travel during this time.

■ **Figure 4.15** The Suez Canal considerably sped up travel times between the Mediterranean and the Indian Ocean

■ **Figure 4.16** Atlantic City at the end of the 19th century. More people were taking holidays as a result of the industrial revolutions

The sea is everything. It covers seven tenths of the terrestrial globe. Its breath is pure and healthy. It is an immense desert, where man is never lonely, for he feels life stirring on all sides. The sea is only the embodiment of a supernatural and wonderful existence. It is nothing but love and emotion; it is the Living Infinite.

Jules Verne, *Twenty Thousand Leagues Under the Sea*

I see that it is by no means useless to travel, if a man wants to see something new.

Jules Verne, *Around the World in 80 Days*

In spite of the opinions of certain narrow-minded people, who would shut up the human race upon this globe, as within some magic circle it must never outstep, we shall one day travel to the moon, the planets, and the stars, with the same facility, rapidity, and certainty as we now make the voyage from Liverpool to New York!

Jules Verne, *From the Earth to the Moon*

■ **Figure 4.17** Jules Verne

▼ **Links to: Language and literature**

Read through the quotations by Jules Verne. What influence do you think writers have on people's sense of adventure and exploration? Can you think of other examples?

REFLECTION

Why do you think the industrialization of nations would affect exploration and travel?

What examples are there of famous female explorers?

There have been many famous explorers throughout history. Here is a small selection of female explorers who made history with their achievements.

ISABELLA BIRD

Facts
English explorer, writer, photographer and naturalist (1831–1904)

Achievements
Travelled all over the world during the nineteenth century. She wrote books about her adventures in the USA, Japan and China.

AMELIA EARHART

Facts
American aviation pioneer and author (1897–1937)

Achievements
First woman to fly solo across the Atlantic. She received the US Distinguished Flying Cross for this record. She disappeared when flying over the Pacific Ocean in 1937.

VALENTINA TERESHKOVA

Facts
Russian cosmonaut (born 1937)

Achievements
In 1963 she was the first woman to travel in space.

■ Figure 4.18 Female explorers

NELLIE BLY

Facts
American journalist (1864–1922)

Achievements
Inspired by *Around the World in 80 Days*, she set out to travel around the world in less time. She successfully made it around the world in 72 days.

ANNIE LONDONDERRY

Facts
Latvian-born explorer (1870–1947)

Achievements
First woman to circle the globe on a bicycle in the late nineteenth century.

ACTIVITY: How have explorers affected the world?

■ ATL

Information literacy skills – Access information to be informed and to inform others

In this summative assessment task you need to choose two explorers and write a report of how they have affected the world. For instance, you might choose Christopher Columbus and Marco Polo and write about the significance of their explorations.

You will need to create a research question for your report that will provide you with a focus. Take a look at the guidance on page 93 on formulating research questions. You should also submit an action plan with your report. The report should be 500–800 words in length. Within your action plan you should keep a record of your research notes as well as planning the time frame of the piece of work.

Finally, remember to include a bibliography at the end of your writing that shows your sources and make references within your writing. If you need reminding how to do this, have a look at *MYP Individuals and Societies 1: By Concept*, Chapter 5, page 113.

Checklist for this task:
- **Research question**
- **Action plan**
- **Written report with references (500–800 words)**
- **Bibliography**

◆ Assessment opportunities

In this activity you have practised skills that are assessed using Criterion A: Knowing and understanding (strands i and ii), Criterion B: Investigating (strands i, ii and iii) and Criterion C: Communicating (strands i, ii and iii).

What examples are there of exploration in the 21st century?

The world is still full of remote places that continue to be explored in order to understand new environments, and to discover new species of animals and plants.

For instance, ocean exploration is a major field of study that is still bringing about new discoveries. In particular, new technology is allowing the depths of the oceans to be explored and mapped.

Remote rainforests, deserts and mountains continue to inspire people to explore and find out more about the world.

Finally, there is of course the matter of space exploration. Beginning in the 20th century, space exploration has become a major global ambition with cooperation between nations enabling the development of new technology and the launch of new expeditions. The significance of the Moon landings in the late 1960s should not be underestimated as a landmark moment in the history of human achievement. At present there are plans to send people to Mars and potentially build the capacity for human life outside of Earth. This shows the extent to which exploration remains an important thread through human history.

■ **Figure 4.19** Exploration and risk: cave diving

■ **Figure 4.20** The Moon landing in 1969 was a turning point in the history of exploration

▼ Links to: Sciences

Mission to Mars

Take a look at the NASA website that discusses the plans for journeys to Mars: www.nasa.gov/content/nasas-journey-to-mars

Discuss the implications of this.

Why do you think the work of NASA would require people to draw upon different disciplines of study? What type of knowledge and understanding would be required to make these types of projects a reality?

4 How does exploration affect global interactions?

REFLECTION: 3, 2, 1 bridge

Individually, on sticky notes or paper, write down:

3 thoughts and ideas

2 questions

1 analogy

… about the word 'exploration'.

This task is repeated from the beginning of the chapter to reflect upon how your understanding of the term 'exploration' has changed as a result of the work completed.

! Take action

Idea 1

! Create a class project based on exploration in your local area. Using maps and your teacher's guidance, plan your own exploration. This could be to find out about some historic buildings or natural environment in your locality.

! You might want to think about the following:
- Where do you want to go?
- Why have you chosen that particular area?
- Do you need any special equipment?
- What is the best way to record information about your exploration?

! Write up a reflection when you finish.

Idea 2

! International Women's Day is on 8 March every year. Famous female explorers and adventurers could be used as a class topic to research. Examples could then be presented in an exhibition or assembly format.

! You might also want to consider why it is important to think about female explorers in particular. What obstacles did they face and how did they overcome them? Could any woman have chosen to become an explorer?

Reflection

In this chapter, we have looked at the different ways that the world has been explored, focusing on the impact that this exploration has had on the world. Exploration has been and continues to be an important part of the human story.

Use this table to reflect on your own learning in this chapter.					
Questions we asked	Answers we found	Any further questions now?			
Factual: How did exploration affect early societies? What were the causes and consequences of the 'Age of Exploration'? How did industrialization affect exploration? What examples are there of female explorers? What examples are there of exploration in the 21st century?					
Conceptual: Why do people explore? What are the causes and consequences of exploration?					
Debatable: Does exploration lead to exploitation?					
Approaches to learning you used in this chapter	Description – what new skills did you learn?	How well did you master the skills?			
		Novice	Learner	Practitioner	Expert
Communication skills					
Information literacy skills					
Critical-thinking skills					
Learner profile attribute(s)	Reflect on the importance of being a risk-taker for your learning in this chapter.				
Risk-takers					

Time, place and space • Resources • Scientific and technical innovation

5 How can energy be produced sustainably?

Humans use **resources** in different ways **around the world**, and use **innovative** methods to be sustainable.

CONSIDER THESE QUESTIONS:

Factual: What are natural resources? What are human and economic resources? What are the differences between renewable, non-renewable and sustainable resources?

Conceptual: What are the arguments for and against different sources of energy production?

Debatable: Is wind power a viable option?

Now **share and compare** your thoughts and ideas with your partner, or with the whole class.

■ **Figure 5.1** Wind power, solar power and water power

IN THIS CHAPTER, WE WILL ...

- **Find out** about the use of resources around the world.
- **Explore** how energy is produced by different resources and the opportunities and challenges associated with this.
- **Take action** by looking at sustainable approaches to energy usage in our local communities.

Individuals and Societies for the IB MYP 2: *by Concept*

These Approaches to Learning (ATL) skills will be useful …

- Communication skills
- Information literacy skills
- Critical-thinking skills

We will reflect on this learner profile attribute …

- **Reflective** – by exploring the values and limitations of different sources of energy production.

Assessment opportunities in this chapter:

- **Criterion C**: Communicating
- **Criterion D**: Thinking critically

KEY WORDS

finite
fossil fuel
geothermal
non-renewable
power
renewable
resources

In this chapter, we will explore the uses of different resources in the world to produce energy. We will gain an understanding of the difference between natural resources and human/economic resources. Case studies will be used to explore the arguments for and against different sources of energy production.

THINK–PAIR–SHARE

How is energy produced?

Create a list of the different ways from your own knowledge. Share with a partner and then feed back your ideas to the class.

5 How can energy be produced sustainably?

What are natural resources?

Natural resources can be found all over the world. They are things that are provided by the Earth. They range from valuable metals through to different gases and their uses vary as well. Natural resources also include plants, sunlight and animals. Humans have been making use of natural resources since prehistoric times. Something as simple as making a fire involved the use of wood, an important natural resource. Using stone to make tools is another early example of resource use.

Natural resources can be categorized as either **biotic** or **abiotic**. Biotic means they are living or derived from living things, so would include plants, animals and fossil fuels. Fossil fuels include coal, oil and natural gas. Abiotic resources originate from non-living things and include different metals such as copper.

The use of natural resources has gradually increased over time as the world population has grown and the technical capacity for resource extraction has become more sophisticated.

Natural resources can be categorised as renewable, non-renewable or sustainable.

- **Renewable** resources can be used again and again and won't run out, such as wind power.
- **Non-renewable** or finite resources have a limited supply and will eventually run out, such as coal and oil.
- **Sustainable** resources are renewable but need management to ensure that this happens. For example, trees need replanting and fishing stocks should be given time to recover.

Natural resource	Uses
Animals	Food and clothing
Plants	Food (fruit, herbs, vegetables)
Oil, coal, natural gas	Energy/electricity (non-renewable)
Trees	Wood, paper
Water	Energy (renewable), drinking
Metals (e.g. gold, silver, copper)	Jewellery, electronics

■ Table 5.1 Natural resources and their uses

ACTIVITY: What are natural resources?

ATL

Information literacy skills – Access information to be informed and to inform others

1 What is a natural resource?
2 Write down whether the following resources are biotic or abiotic: coal, silver, carrots, trees, mushrooms, iron.
3 Categorize the resources from question 2 as renewable, non-renewable or sustainable.
4 Study Figure 5.2. Are all the countries economically reliant on the export of natural resources? What differences can you see in the map?
5 **Explain** how you think the different resources would affect the economy and identity of the different countries, such as Greenland (food/drink) or China (electronics). Choose a couple of examples to explore in more depth.

Natural resources are used to create products, such as the use of metals in electronic goods. They can also be harnessed to create energy. Figure 5.2 shows the dominant resources exported in different areas of the world.

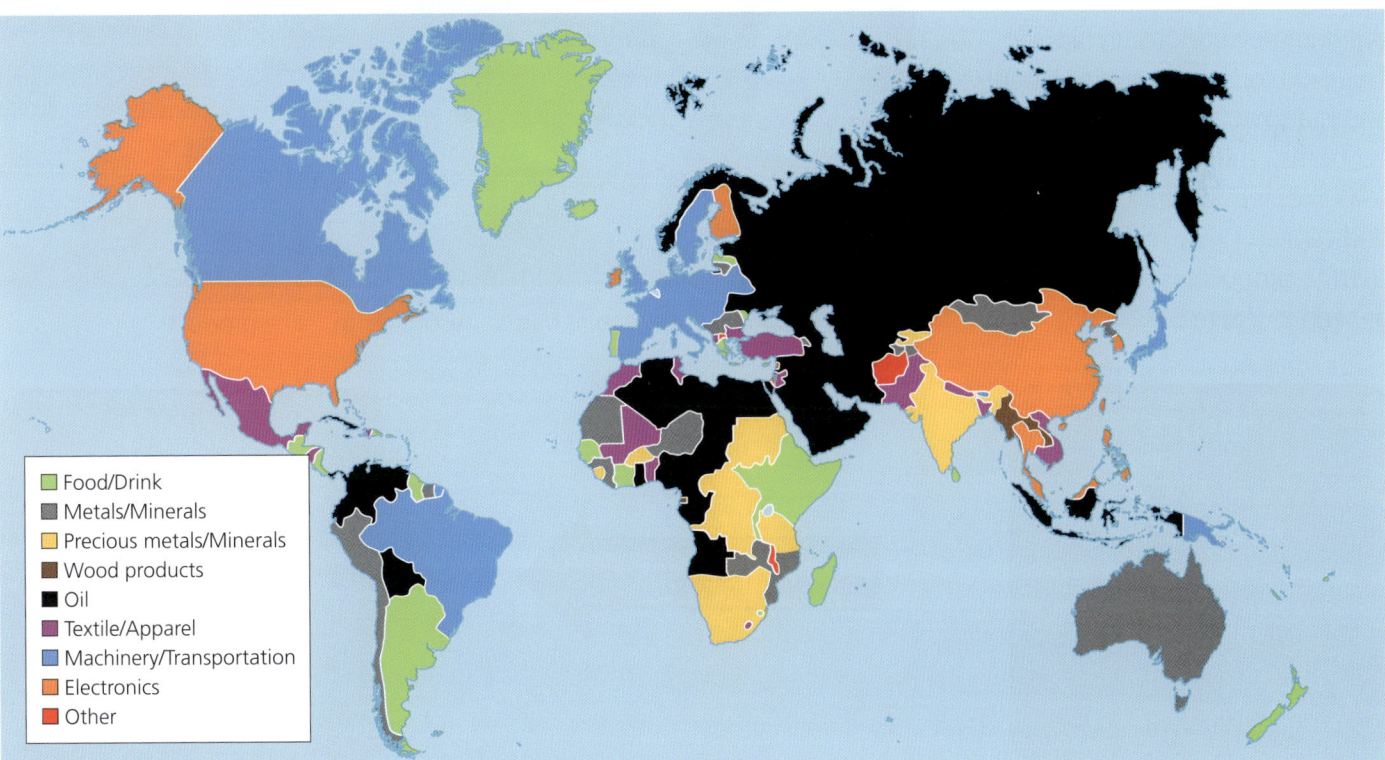

■ **Figure 5.2** The dominant resources exported around the world

5 How can energy be produced sustainably?

What are human and economic resources?

There are also examples of resources in the world that are not naturally occurring. Human and economic resources are important to the economies of the world. Human resources refers to the workforce and the different skills that people have to complete different tasks. For example, factories would not be able to operate if it were not for human resources. Airplanes need well-trained pilots in order for them to fly and surgeons need significant skills in order to perform operations. We would not have food production if it were not for the human workforce in farming. This workforce is known as labour and is also an example of an economic resource. Other economic resources include land, technology and capital. These resources are used to produce a variety of things as seen in Figure 5.4.

■ **Figure 5.3** Factories require human resources to make products

INPUTS
Land
Labour
Capital
Technology
These are human and economic resources

PROCESSES →

OUTPUTS
Food
Buildings
Computers
Plus many more examples

■ **Figure 5.4** Using resources to create products

What are the differences between renewable, non-renewable and sustainable resources?

As mentioned on page 110, resources can be classified as renewable, non-renewable or sustainable.

NON-RENEWABLE ENERGY

The use of resources to generate electricity dates back to the late 19th century when the first power stations were built. Power stations are purpose-built facilities to generate electricity, usually by burning fossil fuels.

Fossil fuels include coal, oil and natural gas. These resources have dominated the production of electricity. Fossil fuels are the remains of living organisms formed millions of years ago, and are a store of energy. When burned, the energy is released and can then be used to generate electricity.

However, there are two key problems with this approach. Firstly, these resources are finite. This means that there is only a limited supply. Eventually these resources will run out. The world has many examples of abandoned coal mines where the supply simply ran out, leaving behind economic uncertainty for the people living in these places. The second major issue is pollution. The burning of these resources leads to excessive amounts of carbon dioxide in the air, which is a major contributor towards global warming and climate change.

Another non-renewable option is nuclear power. Nuclear power stations work in a similar way to power stations that used fossil fuels, in that they generate heat to turn water into steam which then drives turbines to create electricity. The difference is the source of the heat. The heat in nuclear reactors comes from the splitting of uranium atoms. Nuclear power stations generate huge amounts of electricity but they are unpopular as the repercussions of any accident involving nuclear power are very serious. Accidents at Chernobyl in Ukraine in 1986 and Fukushima in Japan in 2011 have made people aware of the dangers of this approach to generating electricity. Despite the dangers, nuclear power does represent an alternative to fossil fuels and is being used increasingly throughout the world.

SOURCE A

Climate scientists predict that if carbon dioxide levels continue to increase, the planet will become warmer in the next century. Projected temperature increases will most likely result in a variety of impacts. In coastal areas, sea-level rise due to the warming of the oceans and the melting of glaciers may lead to the inundation of wetlands, river deltas, and even populated areas. Altered weather patterns may result in more extreme weather events. And inland agricultural zones could suffer an increase in the frequency of droughts.

www.ucsusa.org/clean_energy/our-energy-choices/coal-and-other-fossil-fuels/the-hidden-cost-of-fossil.html#.VxA7ZhOSxSA

SOURCE C

Read the first four paragraphs of this article about a coal-mining town in Colorado.

www.nytimes.com/2015/07/09/us/coal-mine-closed-colorado-town-struggles-to-define-future.html?_r=0

SOURCE B

■ **Figure 5.5** Pollution from a power station

ACTIVITY: Non-renewable resources

■ ATL

Critical-thinking skills – Gather and organize relevant information to formulate an argument

1 According to Source A, what are some of the potential consequences of the increased levels of carbon dioxide in the atmosphere?
2 What do you think are some of the social consequences of the move away from the use of fossil fuels to generate electricity? **Use** Source C and your own knowledge.
3 In groups, copy and complete the following table to argue the benefits and drawbacks of using nuclear power.

Benefits of nuclear power	Drawbacks of nuclear power

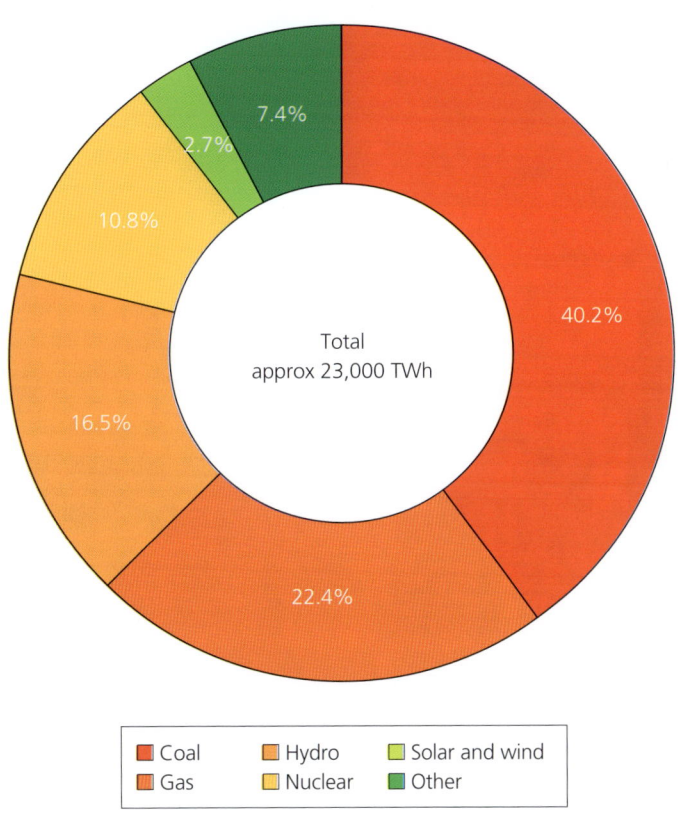

- Coal
- Gas
- Hydro
- Nuclear
- Solar and wind
- Other

Source: IEA Electricity Information 2014

■ **Figure 5.6** World electricity production

DISCUSS

What does the chart in Figure 5.6 tell you about energy production? Write down three conclusions you can come to from the graph.

5 How can energy be produced sustainably?

RENEWABLE ENERGY

An alternative to using non-renewable resources is to use renewable resources to generate energy. Renewable resources are things that can be quickly replaced, for example wind, water and the power of the sun. Harnessing these elements can be very effective in creating large amounts of electricity without damaging the environment.

Renewable energy is very much intertwined with nature. The harnessing of the wind or sunshine poses great opportunities for energy production. It is also sustainable as the supplies will not run out, nor will they pollute the atmosphere. Renewable energy resources include the following:

- **Hydroelectric power** – using running water to generate electricity
- **Solar power** – using sunshine to generate electricity
- **Wind power** – using the wind to power wind turbines
- **Geothermal power** – using heat from the earth to generate electricity

These options are becoming increasingly favourable as nations look for non-polluting methods to generate electricity.

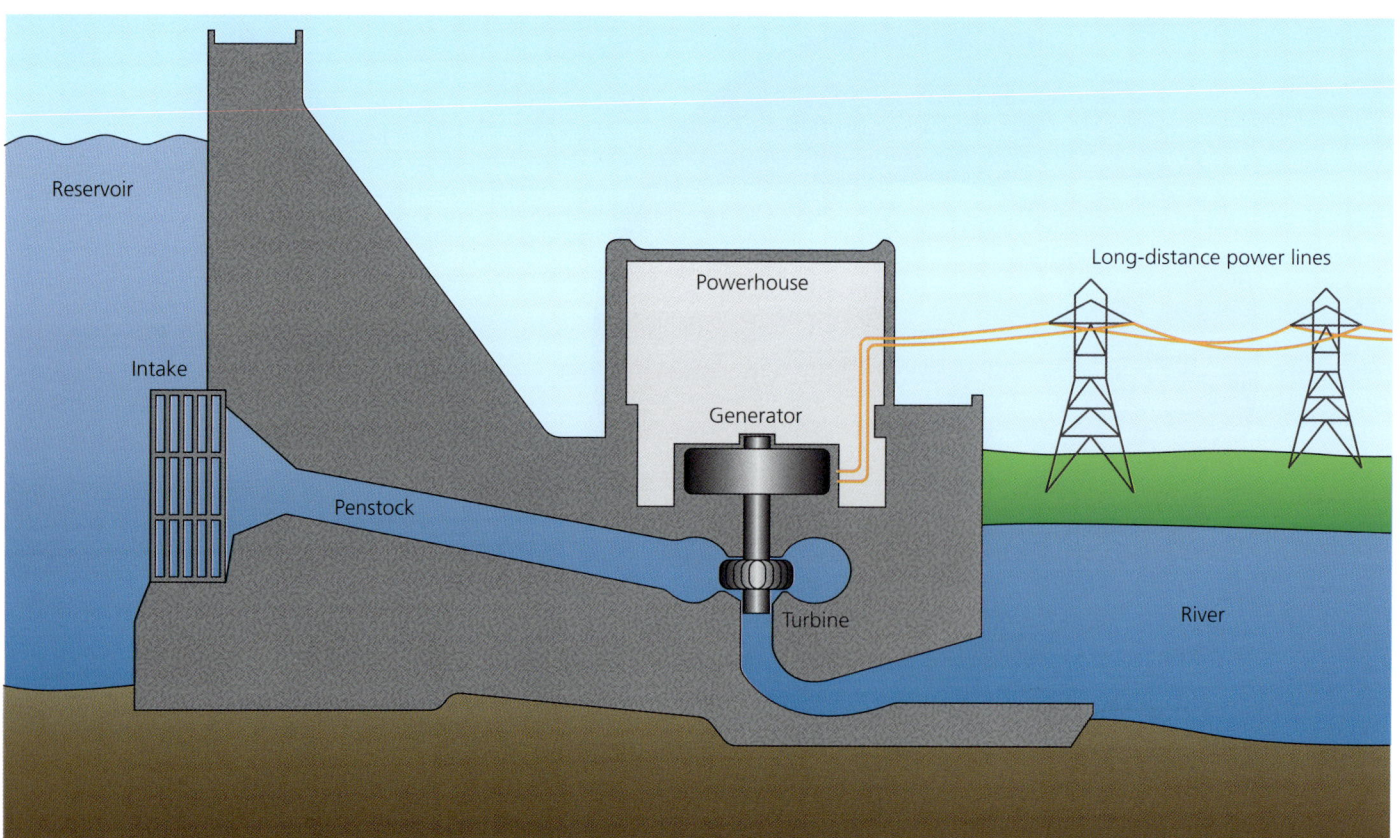

■ **Figure 5.7** A hydroelectric dam

Hydroelectric power

As shown in Figure 5.6, hydroelectric power (HEP) is the most commonly used renewable resource. Hydroelectricity works by releasing large quantities of running water that drive a turbine to generate electricity. Sites that work well for HEP are quite rare as they require the water to move from one elevation to another as shown in Figure 5.7. However, when good sites are found they can yield substantial energy.

CASE STUDY: HYDROELECTRIC POWER – ITAIPU DAM

Itaipu Dam is a hydroelectric dam located on the border of Brazil and Paraguay. Itaipu is the largest hydroelectric power producer in the world. At present there are 20 generator units to produce electricity with an annual output of around 90 terawatt hours (TWh).

The dam generates significant energy for Brazil and Paraguay. Negotiations between the two nations began in the 1960s about harnessing the power of water to generate electricity, utilizing the natural advantages that the countries have. Construction work on the dam began in the early 1970s and in recent decades, extra electric generation units have been added to gradually increase the power output of Itaipu Dam.

The building of the dam led to the displacement of thousands of families as the project required a major restructuring of the area. The creation of the reservoir and dam also had environmental costs, including the destruction of Guaira Falls in order to complete the project.

■ Figure 5.8 Itaipu is on the border of Brazil and Paraguay

■ Figure 5.9 The Itaipu Dam

5 How can energy be produced sustainably?

Solar power

Solar power harnesses the Sun's energy to create electricity through the use of solar panels. These panels convert the Sun's energy into electricity and they are often attached to the roofs of buildings. Buildings therefore can be self-sufficient in terms of their electricity use if they receive enough sunlight. Solar therefore works well in more localised settings as it does not generate the same levels of electricity as hydroelectric power, for example. Solar power has great potential in countries that receive large amounts of sunshine. It is also pollution free.

■ **Figure 5.10** House with solar panels attached to the roof

■ **Figure 5.11** Countries that receive large amounts of sunshine could benefit from solar power

Wind power

A third renewable option for generating energy is by using the power of the wind. This is done through the construction of large wind turbines (similar to windmills) where the turning motion of the rotor blades allows for the creation of energy. Many of these wind turbines are needed to gain decent supplies of electricity and their appearance has been criticised. Despite these concerns, technology is increasingly improving the efficiency of the turbines and their green potential is clearly significant. Wind farms can be constructed offshore so that they are out of the way. After initially being expensive to set up they are typically cheap to run and maintain.

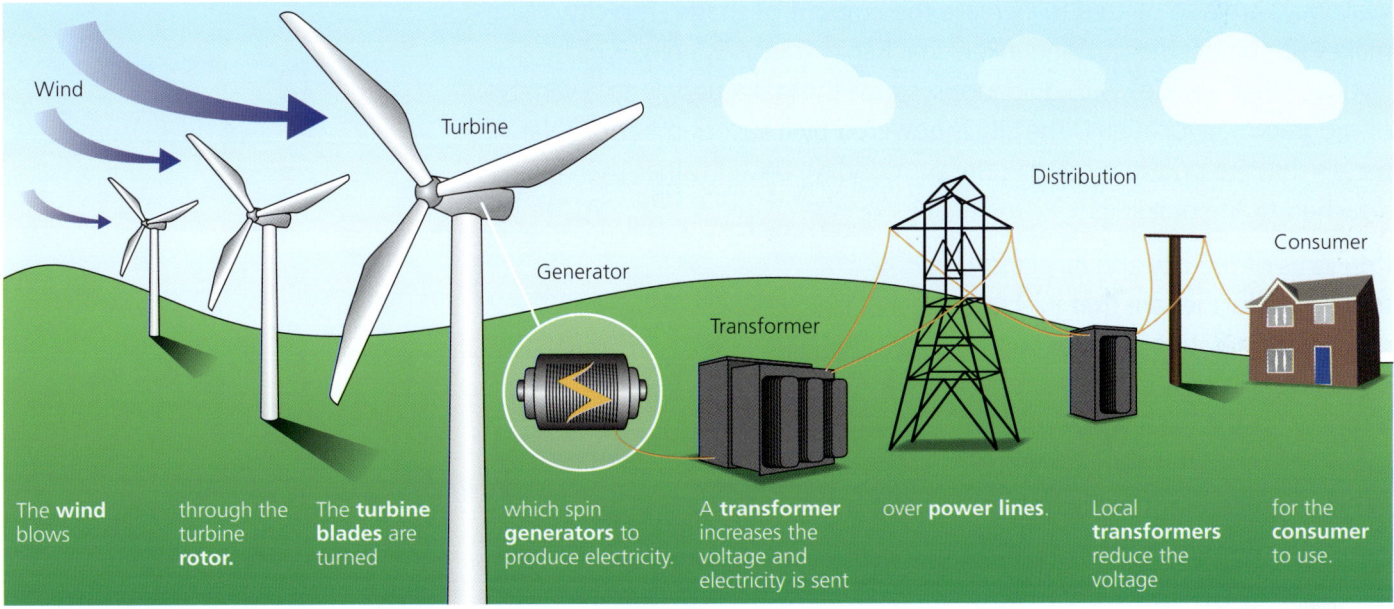

■ **Figure 5.12** How do wind turbines generate electricity?

CASE STUDY: MASDAR CITY

Masdar City is in Abu Dhabi in the United Arab Emirates. It is an experimental development that began in 2006 with the aim of becoming a zero-carbon city with a diversity of renewable energy uses. Although plans have been modified, the city is a good example of how renewable energy can be incorporated into designs. The city hosts the headquarters of the International Renewable Energy Agency.

The city uses traditional designs within its architecture. The designs allow the city to be cooler than the surrounding desert. A large wind tower is used to cool the streets, making the temperature significantly lower. Walkways are also utilized to increase the amount of shade. The city makes use of electric cars and a Personal Rapid Transit System, which involves small vehicles with guidance systems that take people to a variety of programmed locations. The city is powered by a vast number of solar panels that are on the ground in the surrounding desert rather than being attached to the buildings.

Criticisms of the city and its plans to develop further are that it lacks a practical application in other parts of the world and is potentially only a facility for the wealthy. Despite these criticisms, the commitment to environmentally friendly systems makes it a model for development of other cities in the future.

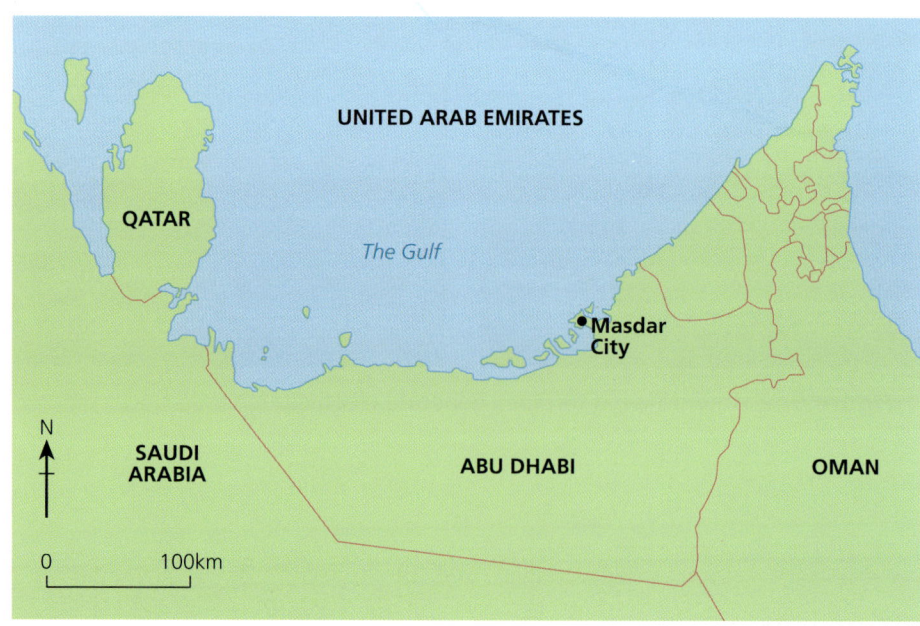

■ Figure 5.13 Masdar City

■ **Figure 5.14** The Personal Rapid Transit System in Masdar City

■ **Figure 5.15** A wind tower in Masdar City

ACTIVITY: Postcard from Masdar City

■ ATL

- Communication skills – Write for different purposes

Imagine that you have been to Masdar City to experience the new technology and the use of renewable resources to generate energy.

Use the information in this book and do some further research. Write a postcard to a friend telling them about Masdar City and what it is like. **Describe** some of the scientific and technological innovations that you have observed.

◆ Assessment opportunities

This activity can be assessed using Criterion C: Communicating (strands i and ii).

5 How can energy be produced sustainably?

Geothermal power

Geothermal power involves the use of the heat from the earth. Volcanic areas, such as Iceland, are the most favourable for this to be practical. The heated rocks under the Earth's crust are used to heat water and produce steam which is used to drive turbines. This is a renewable resource as there is a constant source of heat and pollution does not occur when this method is used.

The disadvantages of geothermal energy are that the number of sites are limited and the dangers of volcanic or earthquake disturbances in these areas can be a threat. New technologies are allowing geothermal energy to be created in the home by using a pump to push cold water down into the ground and have the heated water rise up to generate small quantities of electricity.

> ### DISCUSS
> Why do you think volcanic areas are best for geothermal energy production? What other countries or locations might also be good for geothermal energy production?

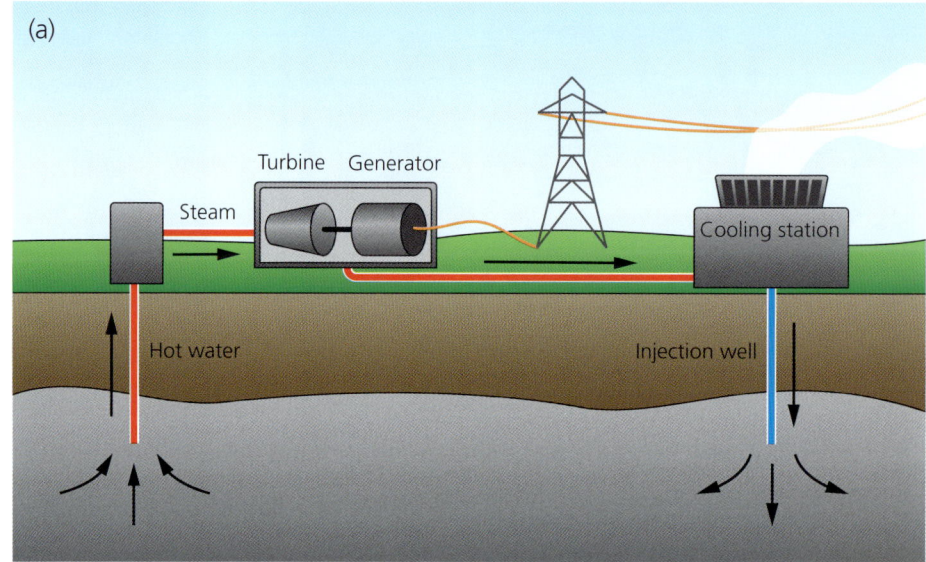

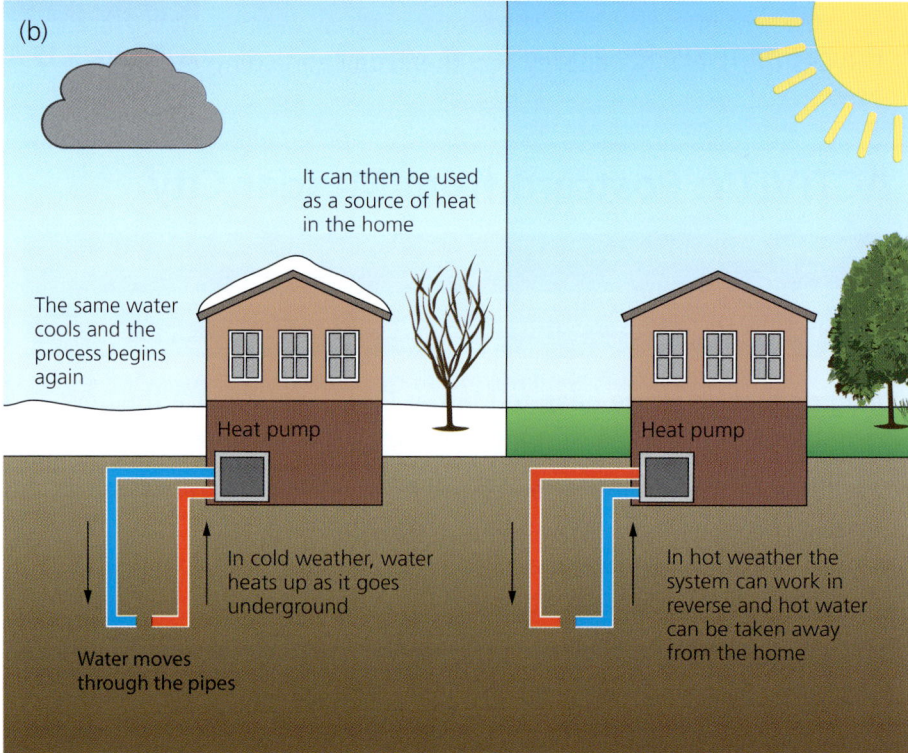

■ **Figure 5.16** (a) A geothermal power plant and (b) geothermal energy in the home

■ **Figure 5.17** Geothermal activity in Iceland

ACTIVITY: Renewable energy

What are the arguments for and against different sources of energy production?

■ ATL

Critical-thinking skills – Evaluate evidence and arguments

1 Read through the explanations and diagrams about the different types of renewable energy and then copy and complete the table below.

Renewable energy source	Advantages	Disadvantages
Hydroelectric		
Solar		
Wind		
Geothermal		

2 Your local government currently relies on a coal-burning power station for its electricity needs. Where you live there is a suitable site for a hydroelectric power station. Write a letter to the government persuading it to investigate this option. Think about the different reasons why it would be a good idea to invest in this project.

◆ Assessment opportunities

In this activity you have practised skills that are assessed using Criterion C: Communicating (strands i and ii) and Criterion D: Thinking critically (strand ii).

REFLECTION

What do you think are some of the main opportunities and challenges associated with the production of energy?

5 How can energy be produced sustainably?

Is wind power a viable option?

SOURCE A

Extract about the economic benefits of wind power from the Greenpeace website, an environmental action group

Generating electricity from the wind makes economic as well as environmental sense. The costs of onshore wind energy fell fourfold in the 1980s, and halved again in the 1990s through a combination of innovation and economies of scale.

As world fossil fuel prices rise and become more volatile as reserves diminish, wind power can help insulate the economy and individuals from those price shocks. For example, the cost of electricity from gas turbine plants in the UK has almost doubled since 2006.

But to get the full benefits of jobs and economic development we need our own wind energy industry – designing and making turbines, erecting and running them.

www.greenpeace.org.uk/

SOURCE B

■ Figure 5.18 Cartoon by Joe Heller

SOURCE C

Extract about wind power from the Union of Concerned Scientists, USA

Sound and visual impact are the two main public health and community concerns associated with operating wind turbines. Most of the sound generated by wind turbines is aerodynamic, caused by the movement of turbine blades through the air. There is also mechanical sound generated by the turbine itself. Overall sound levels depend on turbine design and wind speed.

Some people living close to wind facilities have complained about sound and vibration issues, but industry and government-sponsored studies in Canada and Australia have found that these issues do not adversely impact public health. However, it is important for wind turbine developers to take these community concerns seriously by following 'good neighbor' best practices for siting turbines and initiating open dialogue with affected community members.

www.ucsusa.org/

SOURCE D

Extract from Stanford University website, an academic site

The advantages of wind energy are more apparent than the disadvantages. The main advantages include an unlimited, free, renewable resource (the wind itself), economic value, maintenance cost, and placement of wind harvesting facilities. First and foremost, wind is an unlimited, free, renewable resource. Wind is a natural occurrence and harvesting the kinetic energy of wind doesn't affect currents or wind cycles in any way. Next, harvesting wind power is a clean, non-polluting way to generate electricity. Unlike other types of power plants, it emits no air pollutants or greenhouse gases. The wind turbines harmlessly generate electricity from wind passing by. Wind energy is far more ecofriendly than the burning of fossil fuels for electricity.

http://large.stanford.edu/courses/2014/ph240/lloyd2/

SOURCE E

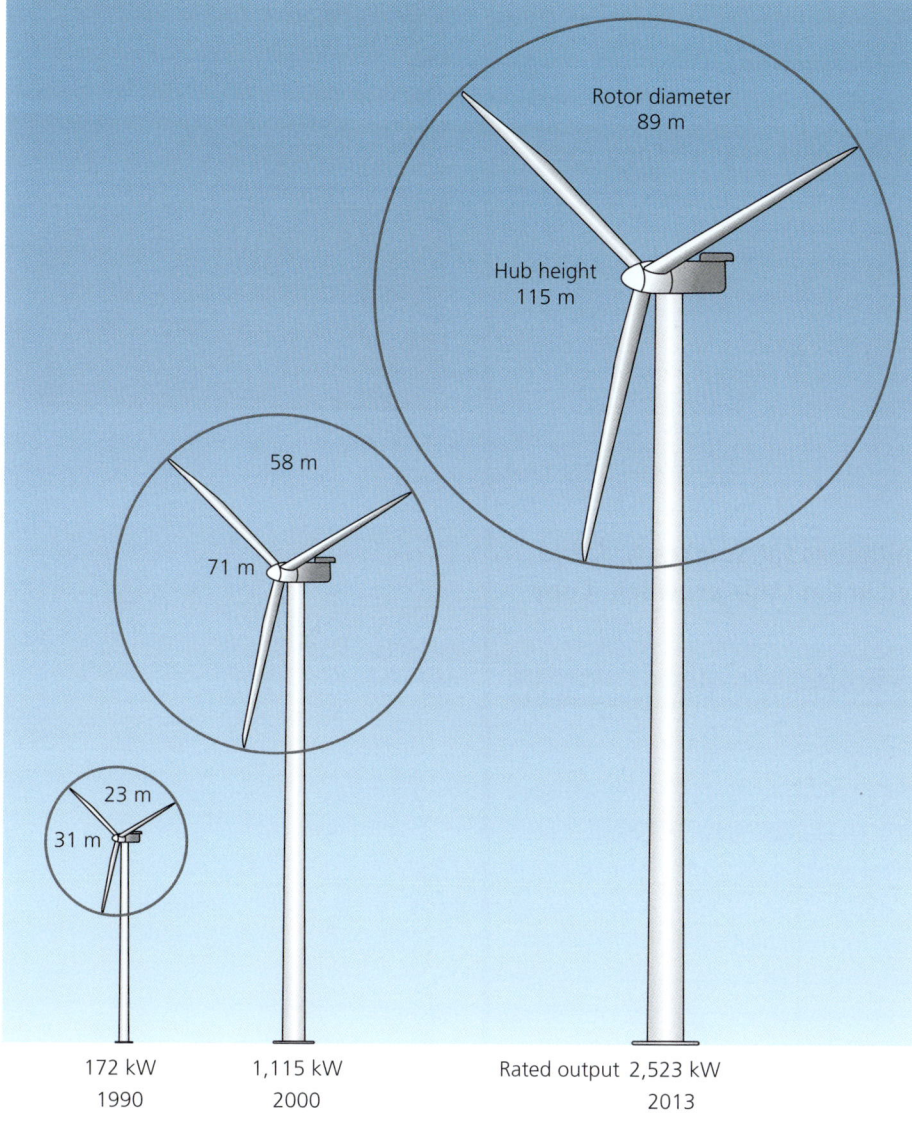

Figure 5.19 Wind turbines

SOURCE F

Extract from the German news website Der Spiegel

Michael Succow, a prominent German environmentalist and winner of the Alternative Nobel Prize, is also threatening to abandon ship. He fears soulless stretches of land and lost tranquility.

And his fears are not unfounded. Back in the 1980s, tree-huggers put up Aeroman wind turbines in their front yards – but those days are long gone. Just the masts of today's wind turbines can reach up to 160 meters high. When active, they kill so many insects that the sticky mass slows the rotors down.

The sweeping blades of the Enercon E-126 cover an area of seven football fields. The rotors of modern wind turbines weigh up to 320 metric tons. There are 83 such three-armed bandits in Germany's largest wind farm, near the village of Ribbeck, northwest of Berlin.

As they drive their SUVs through these turbine forests, tolerantly minded city-dwellers sometimes comment on how ugly eastern Germany has become. Others find them attractive – as they speed past.

But local Nimbies (Nimby = Not In My Back Yard) are indignant. Apart from everything else, the value of their homes has plummeted.

www.spiegel.de/international/germany/wind-energy-encounters-problems-and-resistance-in-germany-a-910816.html

ACTIVITY: Is wind power a viable option?

ATL

Critical-thinking skills – Evaluate evidence and arguments

What are the arguments for and against different sources of energy production?

This activity could be completed in timed conditions.

1 According to the Sources on pages 124–125, what are three advantages and three disadvantages of wind power? Copy and complete the table.

Advantage 1	
Advantage 2	
Advantage 3	
Disadvantage 1	
Disadvantage 2	
Disadvantage 3	

2 What is the message of Source B?
3 Outline the purpose, values and limitations for Sources A, C and D with reference to the origin stated in the table provided. Copy and complete the table.

Source	Origin	Purpose	Value	Limitation
A	Extract about the economic benefits of wind power from the Greenpeace website, an environmental action group			
C	Extract about wind power from the Union of Concerned Scientists, USA, a group of scientists who monitor governmental policies towards the use of scientific developments			
D	Extract from the Stanford University website			

4 'The advantages outweigh the disadvantages.' To what extent do you agree with this statement in regard to the use of wind power to generate electricity? Use the sources and your own knowledge.

◆ Assessment opportunities

In this activity you have practised skills that are assessed using Criterion C: Communicating (strands i and ii) and Criterion D: Thinking critically (strands ii, iii and iv).

! Take action

! Work with a team to reduce the carbon footprint of your school community. What environmental actions could everyone take to reduce your energy usage? For example, switching off lights when you leave a room. Promote your ideas and take action to make your school more energy efficient.

Reflection

In this chapter, we have inquired into the uses of natural resources to produce energy. We have seen that energy is produced through a combination of renewable and non-renewable options. Finally, we have reflected upon the advantages and disadvantages of different renewable energy sources.

Use this table to reflect on your own learning in this chapter.					
Questions we asked	Answers we found	Any further questions now?			
Factual: What are natural resources? What are human and economic resources? What are the differences between renewable, non-renewable and sustainable resources?					
Conceptual: What are the arguments for and against different sources of energy production?					
Debatable: Is wind power a viable option?					
Approaches to learning you used in this chapter	Description – what new skills did you learn?	How well did you master the skills?			
		Novice	Learner	Practitioner	Expert
Communication skills					
Information literacy skills					
Critical-thinking skills					
Learner profile attribute(s)	Reflect on the importance of being reflective for your learning in this chapter.				
Reflective					

Change | Causality; innovation and revolution | Personal and cultural expression

6 How have innovations and ideas changed the world?

Innovations and ideas are developed by a **variety of causes** and can bring about **lasting change** to **individuals and societies**.

CONSIDER THESE QUESTIONS:

Factual: What innovation and ideas came about from the Renaissance? Who were the significant individuals of the Renaissance? What were some of the important changes that occurred during the Enlightenment?

Conceptual: What is an idea or innovation? What makes an innovation or idea significant?

Debatable: Does change affect everyone?

Now **share and compare** your thoughts and ideas with your partner, or with the whole class.

■ Figure 6.1 What makes an idea?

IN THIS CHAPTER, WE WILL …

- **Find out** about examples of ideas and innovations from history.
- **Explore** the time periods of the Renaissance and the Enlightenment and look at some of the main ideas and innovations.
- **Take action** by looking at how ideas and innovations can solve issues in our local communities.

128 — Individuals and Societies for the IB MYP 2: *by Concept*

■ **Figure 6.2** Some ideas have the power to change the way we live. Can you think of any other ideas that have changed the world?

■ These Approaches to Learning (ATL) skills will be useful …
- Communication skills
- Critical-thinking skills

● We will reflect on this learner profile attribute …
- **Inquirer** – by providing opportunities for inquiry into the history of ideas and innovations.

◆ Assessment opportunities in this chapter:
- **Criterion A**: Knowing and understanding
- **Criterion B**: Investigating
- **Criterion C**: Communicating
- **Criterion D**: Thinking critically

KEYWORDS
ideas	perspective
innovation	vaccination

Ideas are funny things. Invisible and weightless, they have no material substance, yet they have the power to change the course of history. Or as the French writer Victor Hugo put it: 'One can resist invading armies; one cannot resist an invasion of ideas.'

Extract from *Time, 100 Ideas That Changed the World*

THINK–PAIR–SHARE
In pairs **discuss** the following questions.
- What is an idea?
- What is an innovation?
- Why are they important?
- Can you think of any that have changed the world?

Discuss your ideas with each other and then share with the rest of class.

6 How have innovations and ideas changed the world?

What is an idea or innovation?

Throughout history there have been many great breakthroughs that have shown the achievements and capabilities of humanity. These have often started as **ideas** or **innovations**. For example, during the time of ancient civilizations, early versions of the alphabet, codes of law, weaponry, the wheel and the seven-day week were developed. These ancient ideas and innovations have changed over time but their creation led to lasting effects on the world.

Ideas can be defined as a new way of looking at something, as a solution to an existing problem or a new approach. An innovation can be another word for an idea or a product that is new. For example, the invention of the wheel can be seen to be an innovation that brought about lasting change.

In this chapter, we will examine two different historical time periods that are particularly noted for a range of innovations and ideas. These are the **Renaissance** and the **Enlightenment**. These time periods in many ways saw significant examples of progress in many fields including the sciences, arts, education, mathematics and politics.

■ **Figure 6.3** Tablet showing the Ancient Greek alphabet

DISCUSS

Why might it be difficult to know for sure where an idea or innovation came from?

■ **Figure 6.4** The Ljubljana Marshes Wheel

ACTIVITY: Ideas that changed the world

■ ATL

Critical-thinking skills – Gather and organize relevant information to formulate an argument

The following ten ideas were named in an article by Professor of Philosophy Tim Crane at the University of Cambridge as significant for changing the world. Look through the list in groups.

- The computer
- Understanding the solar system
- Democracy
- Communism
- Relativity
- Free market
- Quantum theory
- Evolution
- Feminism
- Human rights

In groups, choose one of the ideas from the list. Research it and briefly present your findings to the class, including why you think the idea is significant.

Discuss how the ideas could be categorized, for example, scientific, technological, political, etc.

Search for **Tim Crane's 10 greatest ideas that changed the world** to read more, and to find out what other people think were the best ideas of all time.

Although the world's oldest wheel has been found in Mesopotamia, the earliest images of wheeled carts were found in Poland and elsewhere in the Eurasian steppes. Some have suggested that due to the immense challenge that the invention of the wheel posed to humankind, it probably happened only once, and spread from its place of origin to other parts of the world. However, others believe it developed independently in separate parts of the world at around the same time. For example, The **Ljubljana Marshes Wheel** is a wooden wheel that was found in the capital of Slovenia in 2002 and was dated to 3150BC. At present, the birthplace of the wheel is said to be either in Mesopotamia or the Eurasian steppes. Although Mesopotamia has the oldest known wheel, linguistic evidence is used to support the claim that the wheel originated in the Eurasian steppes. See more at: www.ancient-origins.net/ancient-technology/revolutionary-invention-wheel-001713#sthash.dtEO77Rt.dpuf

REFLECTION

What makes an idea or innovation significant?

In small groups, brainstorm this question. Think about what makes an idea significant. Can you link to the concept of change?

What innovation and ideas came about from the Renaissance?

WHAT WAS THE RENAISSANCE?

The term 'renaissance' means rebirth. The word has been used to describe the historical time period between approximately 1400 and 1600, though dates vary. The Renaissance was named by Swiss historian Jacob Burckhardt as he saw it as a time of a rediscovery of ancient learning from the Roman and Greek civilizations. Following on from the Middle Ages (which we looked at in Chapter 3), the Renaissance was gradually followed by the Enlightenment, during the 17th and 18th centuries.

The Renaissance saw a rediscovery of learning from the ancient civilizations and this had an effect on many fields from the arts and education to architecture and even the way people viewed and understood the solar system.

The Renaissance as we know it largely began in Italy. At the time, Italy was divided into a number of city states. Each of these states ruled its own affairs and they often came into conflict with each other. A period of peace though, lasting 40 years during the 15th century, allowed many of the city states to flourish. Examples of these states included Rome, Milan, Florence, Venice, Pisa and Genoa.

Each state had its own way of ruling and individual characteristics, for example Rome was ruled by the papacy (the Pope) and Venice was, and still is, a lagoon noted for its waterways and unique character. The city state of Florence was particularly significant for the onset of the Renaissance. Ruled by the Medici family, the city was particularly wealthy and invested lots of money in the arts.

■ **Figure 6.5** The Renaissance began in the Italian city states. Of particular importance was the city state of Florence, which was controlled by the influential Medici family in the 15th century

WHAT WERE THE KEY IDEAS OF THE RENAISSANCE?

Humanism

Humanism essentially was the study of what it means to be a human. It encouraged an interest in studying the human body. This included the anatomy and physiology of the body, which are the parts of the body and how they work together. Humanism also involved a greater degree of individualism and studying the potential of humans in different fields. Humanism in the arts showed more realistic pictures of people, for example the increased use of portraits.

Humanism developed through the rediscovery of books from the classical world of the Greeks and the Romans. The rediscovery of these books happened through a variety of means. The poet Francesco Petrarch was particularly important in this process. An avid book lover, he tracked down numerous books from the Ancient Greeks and Romans which helped to establish the collection of books at the library in Florence. Petrarch and his followers' contributions were significant as they also raised awareness of the main themes of the books, such as the writings of the Roman lawyer Cicero, which helped to develop the idea of humanism.

Classicism

Humanism was accompanied by **classicism**. This is the broad term that refers to the rediscovery of the works of the Greeks and Romans. However, this development had significant practical consequences. Many of the architectural styles of the Greeks and Romans were brought back during the Renaissance. Examples included the arch, the dome, columns and pediments. In addition, classicism also saw renewed interest in some of the political dimensions of the ancient world. Ancient Greek systems of government that promoted democratic measures were looked at with interest.

> ### DISCUSS
> Why do you think Petrarch's discoveries of Ancient Greek and Roman books was important to the Renaissance?

> ### DISCUSS
> What aspects of humanism and classicism can you see in Figure 6.7?

■ **Figure 6.6** Francesco Petrarch

■ **Figure 6.7** Classicism in art: Perugino's 'Delivery of the Keys'

■ **Figure 6.8** (a) A medieval painting of a lion, (b) a Renaissance painting of a lion

Perspective

Within the arts, the challenge of creating more realistic works of art was taken on during the Renaissance. During the Middle Ages, much of the artwork was not of realistic proportions. Renaissance artists wanted to represent 3D shapes more realistically on a 2D canvas.

One technique that was developed was called 'chiaroscuro', which involved the use of light and shade for a more realistic image. The use of a 'vanishing point' within a work of art also helped to increase the sense of perspective. The achievements of the Renaissance artists and architects in the creation of more realistic drawings also advanced the ability to design and build complex structures. It was not until the invention of photography that visual representation became a much simpler process.

DISCUSS

What differences can you see in the portrayal of the lion in the two different images in Figure 6.8? Which one do you think is using perspective?

Natural world

Another preoccupation of the Renaissance was the natural world. This was reflected in the arts where landscapes were drawn showing a range of natural scenery.

■ **Figure 6.9** The 'Mona Lisa', one of the most famous artworks from the Renaissance period

■ **Figure 6.10** Basilica di Santa Maria del Fiore. The dome was a particular architectural achievement during the Renaissance

DISCUSS

Why can the 'Mona Lisa' be seen as an example of humanism, perspective and the natural world within the arts?

THINK–PAIR–SHARE

Consider the debatable question 'Does change affect everyone?' in connection with the examples from the Renaissance. Do you think developments in the arts would affect everyone? Which groups in society were likely to experience these changes?

Discuss in pairs and then feed back your ideas.

Who were the significant individuals of the Renaissance?

The Italian city states were where much of the Renaissance took place. These included the city states of Florence, Milan and Venice. The city states were very wealthy, so people were able to pursue many of the important ideas of the Renaissance. Florence in particular was of significance: ruled by the powerful Medici family, it was at the centre of many of the developments during the Renaissance. This also included the work of significant individuals, Leonardo Da Vinci and Michelangelo.

Leonardo Da Vinci

Leonardo Da Vinci is regarded by many as the ultimate example of a 'Renaissance man'. This term refers to someone who is highly skilled in many different areas of their life, and is well educated and virtuous. The term 'Renaissance man' was coined during the time period by humanists who were looking at the ways that people could improve themselves.

Da Vinci was born in 1452 and among his many famous works, the 'Mona Lisa', the 'Vitruvian Man' and 'The Last Supper' are perhaps the best known. Among other things, Da Vinci focused much of his attention on the study of human anatomy. Anatomy refers to the different parts of the human body such as the skeleton, organs and muscles. He was also interested in religious imagery as seen in 'The Last Supper'. Da Vinci was in many ways a visionary, with his drawings including sketches of helicopters and bicycles. Subsequently he has been credited with designing many things that became a reality much later on in time. Leonardo Da Vinci died in 1519.

■ **Figure 6.11** Leonardo Da Vinci

136   Individuals and Societies for the IB MYP 2: *by Concept*

Michelangelo

A second Renaissance man, Michelangelo lived from 1475 to 1564. He is famous for his sculptures and he also painted the famous works of art on the ceiling of the Sistine Chapel in Rome. Michelangelo grew up in Florence and was taught by many of the best artists and sculptors. This led to his famous sculptures 'Pietà' and 'David', which showed the influence of the Classical era.

■ **Figure 6.12** Michelangelo's sculpture of David

> ## EXTENSION
>
> ### Contrasting viewpoints: The ideal leader
>
> The humanists proposed a 'Renaissance man', someone who was well educated and mannered and a good leader. Different perspectives came about as to what a good leader looked like.
>
> An interesting perspective on leadership can be found in Nicholas Machiavelli's book *The Prince*. Machiavelli had observed the different leadership styles of the Italian city states and for a time he was imprisoned and tortured in Florence by the Medici family. In his book *The Prince*, Machiavelli makes the case that a good leader would use power skilfully. This would include using terror when necessary to wipe out opposition. His proposition that leaders should not take moral responsibility can be seen as a dangerous viewpoint.
>
> From *The Prince*:
>
> > 'Everyone sees what you appear to be, few experience what you really are.'
>
> > 'If an injury has to be done to a man it should be so severe that his vengeance need not be feared.'
>
> ## DISCUSS
>
> What do you think? What characteristics do you think make a good leader?

WHAT OTHER IDEAS AND INNOVATIONS CAME FROM THE RENAISSANCE?

The printing press

The **printing press** was invented by Johannes Gutenberg from Mainz in Germany in 1450. The invention revolutionized access to books for people, as previously books were handwritten and hand drawn, which was a very slow process. Books could be produced more quickly and therefore cheaply, which meant that more people had access to a wider range of books, which subsequently advanced the development of new ideas through the Renaissance. One of the early books to be widely printed was the Gutenberg Bible, which was printed in large numbers.

Advances in astronomy

During the Renaissance there were also important developments in the field of astronomy. The work of Nicolaus Copernicus and Galileo Galilei was of particular importance. Copernicus put forward the theory that the Sun was the centre of the universe rather than the commonly held belief that the Earth was at the centre of the universe. This theory was studied by the Italian scientist and astronomer Galileo, who developed Copernicus' work by observing further details in the solar system, including the moons of Jupiter, as well as supporting the claim that the Earth orbits the Sun. Galileo did this with his invention of an improved version of the telescope, which allowed him and others to observe more details in the night sky.

These advances led to the period described as the Scientific Revolution.

Gutenberg's invention pulled together several different technologies. It combined block printing, a Chinese technique brought to Europe by Marco Polo, with the press used to make wine and olive oil. His great innovation was movable type – sets of letters made out of metal. Instead of having to carve a solid block of wood for every single page, printers could rearrange the letters and reuse the type to print new pages.

Extract from 'How did the Printing Press Change History?' for Junior Scholastic – an educational resource for students

■ **Figure 6.13** Gutenberg's printing press

■ **Figure 6.14** Galileo's telescope

ACTIVITY: Essay on the Renaissance

■ ATL

Communication skills – Write for different purposes

For this task you need to answer the following question:

'The Renaissance led to lasting change in society.' Do you agree with this statement? **Explain** your answer.

Using the information in this chapter and further research, write a response to this question.

You will need to write 400–500 words in paragraphs. Remember to use evidence to support your points and make sure that your answer is balanced.

Find evidence and arguments to both agree and disagree with the statement.

Finally, ensure that your answer has both an introduction and a conclusion.

◆ Assessment opportunities

In this activity you have practised skills that are assessed using Criterion A: Knowing and understanding (strands i and ii), Criterion C: Communicating (strands i, ii and iii) and Criterion D: Thinking critically (strand ii).

Writing essays

Writing essays is an important part of Individuals and societies and is a skill that you need to develop as you go through school. Here is a quick checklist of things to remember when writing an essay. Good luck!

Introduction

- Remember to introduce the question you are answering.
- Provide a hook to get the reader interested in what you are writing.

Body paragraphs

- Use connectives to tie your work together, for example 'subsequently', 'furthermore'.
- Make sure each paragraph has a main point that is supported by evidence and examples.
- Link back to the essay question where appropriate.
- Use a range of evidence, for example dates, facts, statistics, quotations.

Conclusion

- Write your overall answer to the question.
- Be consistent with what you have said in your essay.
- Make it clear.

What were some of the important changes that occurred during the Enlightenment?

The term 'the Enlightenment' refers to a period of time in Europe and America that began in the mid-17th century and lasted throughout the 18th century. This period of time is important to the history of ideas as it saw many changes in the fields of science, philosophy, politics and mathematics. The Enlightenment is sometimes referred to as the 'Age of Reason'. This is because the use of reason became an important way that thinkers of the time approached many questions in their fields of study. **Reason** means to make decisions based on a logical approach, and involves using rational approaches to problems. This was very important to developments in the sciences as many advances were made due to this approach, including the development of the scientific method.

There were also many developments in philosophy and politics. Inspired by humanism during the Renaissance, there were many thinkers during the Enlightenment who raised questions about the world around them. In this section, we will look at the impact of the Enlightenment on science and politics.

DEVELOPMENTS IN SCIENCE

As we have already seen, the Enlightenment was preceded by the Scientific Revolution, when scientists such as Copernicus and Galileo made great discoveries.

Proposing that the Sun was at the centre of the solar system went against the ingrained thinking of the previous centuries and challenged many authorities. It was this spirit of inquiry and questioning which allowed other scientists to make discoveries.

One of the most significant developments during the Enlightenment was the adoption of the scientific method by numerous scientists. It is still in use today.

■ **Figure 6.15** Famous Enlightenment experiment where the American scientist Benjamin Franklin attracted lightning to a metal key attached to a kite to prove that lightning was a type of electricity

Although there were many contributors to the methodology of the scientific method, the work of Francis Bacon was particularly important. He was an English scientist who believed in making observations, collecting data and then, after careful reflection, drawing conclusions. This practice, which emphasizes the importance of observation and testing, is known as **empiricism**.

Influenced by Bacon and others, the **scientific method** came into common usage during the Enlightenment, although versions of it had existed previously. The approach, as shown in Figure 6.16, was a methodical approach to testing predictions and hypotheses in order to come up with usable theories in the sciences.

> 'The scientific method is, I think, one of the greatest gifts of human culture in allowing us to separate myths and dogma from reality.'
> – James Meigs, *Popular Mechanics*

> 'In questions of science, the authority of a thousand is not worth the humble reasoning of a single individual.' – Galileo Galilei

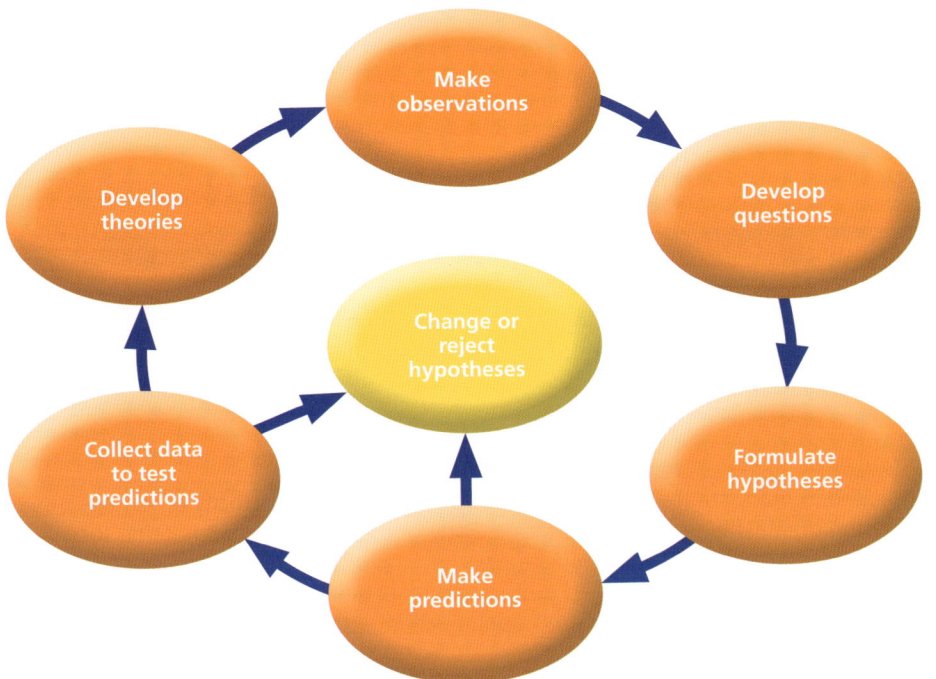

■ **Figure 6.16** The scientific method was developed during the Enlightenment

▼ **Links to: Sciences**

Think about how you might use the scientific method in your science experiments.

ACTIVITY: Source analysis

■ **ATL**

Critical-thinking skills – Evaluate evidence and arguments

Looks at Sources A–C on page 143.

1. According to Source A, why is Isaac Newton an important figure in the field of science?
2. Study Sources B and C. **Discuss** how the clock works to determine longitude. Why do you think it took so long to create this innovation?
3. What do you think changed as a result of the development of Harrison's clock?
4. Copy and complete the **evaluation** table below.

◆ **Assessment opportunities**

This activity can be assessed using Criterion D: Thinking critically (strand iii).

Origin	Purpose	Value	Limitation
Source A Extract about Isaac Newton's achievements from the book *Time: 100 Ideas That Changed the World*, 2010, New York			
Source B Extract about the work of John Harrison on the Open University website **www.open.edu/**			
Source C Photograph of John Harrison's clock that helps determine longitude at sea for sailors			

6 How have innovations and ideas changed the world?

SCIENTIFIC IDEAS AND INNOVATION OF THE ENLIGHTENMENT

Idea or innovation		Description
The scientific method		As discussed already, the new approaches to science in the scientific method showed a much greater emphasis on reasoning and observation. These approaches were important to many breakthroughs in science and are still an important part of the subject today.
Electricity		Developed in many stages over the years. The harnessing of electricity is perhaps one of the greatest innovations of all time. Early pioneers of electricity during the Enlightenment were Otto Von Guericke who developed an electrostatic generator and Benjamin Franklin who worked out how to store electricity, as well identifying the positive and negative charge. It wasn't until much later though that electricity began to be used in the home.
Longitude		Points of the same longitude are connected by the parallel lines running north to south on the globe. For a long time there was no way of calculating longitude at sea, which led to shipwrecks. An English carpenter, John Harrison, solved this problem by using clocks. Greenwich in London became the location of longitude zero and time was measured against the time in London to calculate the number of degrees longitude that had been travelled. John Harrison's clock allowed this complex process to become a reality.
Gravity		A massive breakthrough of the Enlightenment was the discovery of the laws of gravity by the scientist Isaac Newton. This helped to explain the movement of the planets in the solar system. Newton also discovered the laws of motion and invented calculus so his contributions to the fields of science and mathematics are significant.
Encyclopedias		Still popular nowadays, encyclopedias contain vast amounts of information that is accessible for a wide audience. They help people to understand developments in the sciences. During the Enlightenment, scientific knowledge began to be shared in encyclopedias so people could access and figure out the new ideas as they emerged.
Vaccination		Another breakthrough of the Enlightenment was the development by Edward Jenner of vaccination against the deadly disease smallpox (see page 144).

■ Table 6.1 Scientific ideas and innovations

SOURCE A

Extract about Isaac Newton from Time: 100 Ideas That Changed the World

Building upon the work of Galileo and Johannes Kepler, Newton developed his greatest achievement, his universal law of gravity. It states that every physical body attracts every other with a force directly proportional to the product of their masses and inversely proportional to the square of the distance between them. That law made it possible for him to explain the movements of the moon and all the planets, the orbits of comets and even the tides. But he did more. He discovered that light was composed of the full spectrum of colors. He perfected a version of the reflecting telescope … Hugely influential, Newton was more than simply a man of science. He was the very idea of science personified.

SOURCE B

'Harrison's Clock – The Answer At Last'

After decades of diligence, and many design changes, he eventually produced his marine chronometer, H4, a spring-driven clock that could measure longitude to within the half-degree required for the £20,000 prize. Despite this, Harrison was initially awarded only half the promised amount.

On a voyage from England to Jamaica in 1761–62, H4 lost just five seconds in over two months at sea. It was now possible for a navigator to determine local time by measuring high noon, and compare this to the absolute time, which had been set on an accurate chronometer at the start of the voyage. With this information, he could then determine the number of degrees of longitude that he'd traversed during his journey.

At long last, both latitude and longitude could now be determined accurately, and for the first time you could say exactly where on Earth you were.

www.open.edu/

SOURCE C

■ **Figure 6.17** Photograph of Harrison's clock in Greenwich

THE DEVELOPMENT OF VACCINATION

A major breakthrough during the Enlightenment was the development of vaccination. During the 18th century, the smallpox disease was a major cause of death. It led to the body being covered in fluid-filled blisters.

The earlier treatment for smallpox was called variolation. This was a technique that involved people being exposed to a small dose of smallpox in hope that they would catch a mild form of the disease. Variolation sometimes led to death from smallpox so it wasn't the most effective treatment.

An English doctor, Edward Jenner, proposed an alternative to variolation and was able to find a treatment for the disease. Jenner had observed that people who caught the cowpox disease did not tend to catch smallpox; this tended to be milkmaids who worked on farms. Subsequently Jenner developed the idea that exposure to the cowpox disease would protect against smallpox. He tested this by injecting a small amount of cowpox into eight-year-old James Phipps. James caught a mild strain of cowpox and then recovered. Jenner then variolated James Phipps with smallpox and, to his relief, he did not catch smallpox. Jenner had discovered vaccination. Jenner used the scientific method by continually testing this theory on other cases to ensure that he had found a solution to the problem.

Jenner faced widespread opposition from members of the scientific community but eventually his idea won out and this led to the establishment of vaccination as an invaluable form of disease prevention around the world.

SOURCE A

Overview of the work of Edward Jenner

Edward Jenner, born in mid-18th century England, would eventually become one of the most famous scientists in medical history and the so-named 'Father of Immunology.' After observing that cowpox infection seemed to protect humans against smallpox, Jenner inoculated an eight-year-old boy with cowpox matter from a blister on the hand of an English milkmaid. He then repeatedly attempted to 'challenge' the cowpox inoculation by exposing the boy to smallpox material – but the boy never fell ill. Jenner had demonstrated smallpox immunization.

Jenner's method of vaccination against smallpox grew in popularity and eventually replaced variolation, which had been the standard before his demonstration. In the latter part of the 20th century, about 150 years after Jenner's death in 1823, smallpox would be making its last gasps. It would eventually be eradicated after a massive surveillance and vaccination program – thanks largely to the initial efforts of the Father of Immunology.

www.historyofvaccines.org/

SOURCE B

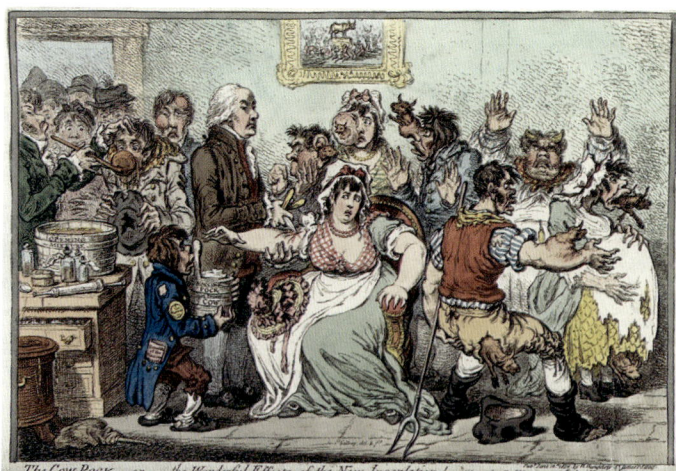

■ **Figure 6.18** Political cartoon showing Jenner delivering the cowpox dose

SOURCE C

Extract about the opposition to vaccination

Soon even political cartoonists, such as James Gillray, were publishing engravings that showed people growing cow's heads on their bodies. People became fearful of the possible consequences of receiving material originating from cows, and opposed vaccination on religious grounds saying that they would not be treated with substances originating from God's lowlier creatures.

Variolation was forbidden by Act of Parliament in 1840, and vaccination with cowpox was made compulsory in 1853. This, in its turn, led to protest marches and vehement opposition from those who demanded freedom of choice.

https://drjennershouse.files.wordpress.com/2016/09/jenner-for-website2.pdf

SOURCE D

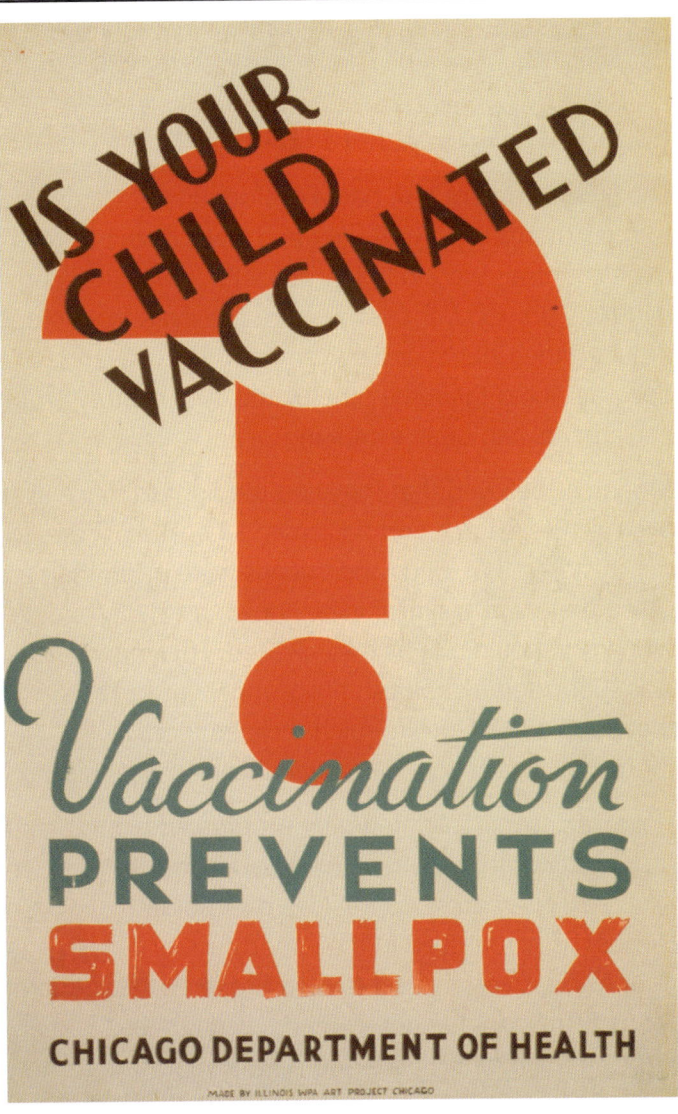

■ **Figure 6.19** Poster promoting vaccination against smallpox

ACTIVITY: Jenner and vaccination

■ **ATL**

Critical-thinking skills – Draw reasonable conclusions and generalizations

1. According to Source A, what is the significance of the work of Edward Jenner?
2. What is the message of Source B?
3. Why do you think there was so much opposition to the idea of vaccination?
4. What is Source D an example of? What role do you think governments have in promoting health?

What changes do you think occurred in the sciences as a result of the earlier Scientific Revolution and the Enlightenment? Do you think any of the changes we have looked at would affect all sections of society?

POLITICS AND THE ENLIGHTENMENT

The Enlightenment also had a profound effect on politics. Politics refers to the systems of government and laws. At the time of the Enlightenment most countries were ruled by absolute monarchs, kings or queens who had total power over their people. The rivals for the power of the monarch included the Church and parliaments. The influence of the Church had been declining for some time by the 18th century and the influence of parliaments had been increasing.

Monarchs believed that they had the right to make all the decisions and overrule the Church and parliaments because of the 'Divine Right of Kings' which stated that kings and queens were given their authority by God. In China there was a similar idea, known as the 'Mandate of Heaven', that emperors should rule as they pleased. The importance of strong authority was supported by a British philosopher called Thomas Hobbes, who stated that people need strong rulers to keep them in line. Hobbes wrote down these ideas in his book *Leviathan* which was published in 1651.

However, as the Enlightenment progressed a number of voices, including those of two philosophers, John Locke and Jean Jacques Rousseau, proposed alternatives to the idea of absolutism. Locke differed from Hobbes as he believed in the importance of certain rights, including the right to life, freedom and to own property. Locke therefore saw the need for more responsible governments and monarchs to ensure that people received a fair deal. Locke praised the importance of equality. Rousseau took these ideas even further, proposing that people were good at heart and that they were corrupted by society. Rousseau famously remarked 'Man is born free but everywhere he is in chains.' Rousseau's book *The Social Contract*, published in 1762, explores these ideas in depth.

The ideas of Locke and Rousseau were to have a profound effect during the revolutions that took place in France and the USA. In France (1789–99), in the spirit of liberty, equality and brotherhood, the absolute monarchy and the system of estates was overthrown. The American War of Independence (1775–83) led to the creation of a newly independent nation, the USA, free from the control of the British crown.

■ **Figure 6.20** Caricature of the pressure placed on the poorer levels of society prior to the French Revolution. Rousseau's *The Social Contract* influenced many thinkers during the time

EXTENSION

Inquire into the historical context of the American and French Revolutions to increase your understanding. The following links can help:

American Revolution Crash Course – https://youtu.be/HlUiSBXQHCw

French Revolution Crash Course – https://youtu.be/lTTvKwCylFY

What makes an innovation or idea significant?

ACTIVITY: Ideas that changed the world

What makes an innovation or idea significant?

ATL

- Communication skills – Use a variety of speaking techniques to communicate with a variety of audiences
- Critical-thinking skills – Gather and organize relevant information to formulate an argument

For the summative task you will need to prepare a five- to seven-minute presentation on one idea or innovation that you think changed the world. It could be an idea from the case studies in this chapter or it could be something else. The list at the start of the chapter (see page 131) can give you some extra ideas.

Within your presentation you will need to do the following:

1. Introduce your idea or innovation.
2. What is the story behind it? How did it come about?
3. Who was involved? Was there any resistance when it came about?
4. Why do you think it changed the world? What is its significance?
5. Provide and **explain** examples of different perspectives on the idea, such as opposition to the idea, different viewpoints on its significance.

A challenging part of this task will be including different perspectives on the idea of your choosing. For example, if you chose vaccination, you could include the perspectives of people who were against vaccination as shown in this chapter. Or, if you were covering political ideas during the Enlightenment, the different viewpoints of philosophers would work. Aim to include two or three different perspectives within your work.

Along with your presentation you will need to submit an action plan that shows your planning and organization as well as an **evaluation** of the presentation.

◆ Assessment opportunities

In this activity you have practised skills that are assessed using Criterion A: Knowing and understanding (strands i and ii), Criterion B: Investigating (strands ii, iii and iv), Criterion C: Communicating (strands i, ii and iii) and Criterion D: Thinking critically (strands ii and iv).

! Take action

! Hold a school or class competition to create an innovation that solves an environmental issue in your community. Think about what some of the issues are and then take action individually or in groups to brainstorm and create a range of solutions.

Reflection

In this chapter, we have inquired into the key concept of change by looking at the ideas and innovations during the Renaissance and the Enlightenment. We have seen how ideas and innovations have shaped changes in the arts, sciences, politics and astronomy.

We should recognize that ideas and innovations have occurred throughout history and will continue to occur into the future with varying degrees of consequence.

Use this table to reflect on your own learning in this chapter.					
Questions we asked	Answers we found	Any further questions now?			
Factual: What innovation and ideas came about from the Renaissance? Who were the significant individuals of the Renaissance? What were some of the important changes that occurred during the Enlightenment?					
Conceptual: What is an idea or innovation? What makes an innovation or idea significant?					
Debatable: Does change affect everyone?					
Approaches to learning you used in this chapter	Description – what new skills did you learn?	How well did you master the skills?			
		Novice	Learner	Practitioner	Expert
Communication skills					
Critical-thinking skills					
Learner profile attribute(s)	How did you demonstrate your skills as an inquirer in this chapter?				
Inquirer					

6 How have innovations and ideas changed the world?

Glossary

altitude the height of a location above sea level

biome a large area of similar flora and fauna and natural environment e.g. a desert

black death a disease which spread through the world in the 14th century, it was the nickname for the bubonic plague

classicism the interest and pursuit of Ancient Greek and Roman learning e.g. in architecture

climate change the process of the Earth's climate changing due to human impact and usage

Columbian Exchange the exchange of goods between the Americas and Europe during the 16th century

consumer within a food web, consumers feed off plants and animals

Dark Ages a historical time period after the fall of the Roman empire in Western Europe where there was a loss of learning and advancement

decomposer within a food web, decomposers are responsible for breaking down dead animals and plants, e.g. mushrooms and certain insects

developing country a country that is looking to become more advanced economically and socially

developed country a country that is considered economically and socially advanced

ecosystem a biological community of interaction organisms

empire a group of countries or states under the control of one authority e.g. British empire

empiricism the idea that knowledge comes from the senses and observation

Enlightenment a historical time period from the mid-17th century through to the end of the 18th century where there were a great many developments in the fields of science, politics and philosophy

exploration travelling in unfamiliar areas to find out new things

feudal system a power structure shaped like a pyramid where owning land gave you power

food web a system of interdependent food chains

foot binding the process of reshaping the foot to make it pointed; this practice used to occur in China

franchise an authorization by a company to run an outlet using the company's specific products

gaucho a cowboy from the Pampas region of South America

globalization the different processes and results of interdependence around the world include trade and communication

globetrotters people with a sense of adventure who travel the world

homage showing respect publicly

humanism an approach that developed during the Renaissance which explored the capacity of human beings in their lives. It influenced the arts

industrialization the development of industries in a particular region

latitude the location of a place North or South of the Equator, usually measured in degrees

maritime effect the effect of the sea or ocean on the climate of nearby land. It cools the land in the summer and warms the land in the winter

Middle Kingdom a name given to China

migration the movement of people (can also refer to animals) from one place to another

nomadic people who travel from place to place and do not permanently settle

ocean currents channels of air that flow over the oceans and affect the climate of other places e.g. the Gulf Stream

printing press developed by Johannes Gutenberg, this invention revolutionized communication and the distribution of books. Books could be mass produced with this invention rather than being written and drawn by hand

producer within a food web, producers are the plants and vegetation that are food to the consumers

reason a logical approach to making decisions

renaissance a historical time period where there was a 'rebirth' in learning from the Ancient Greeks and Romans. This led to developments in many fields including the sciences and the arts. It began in the Italian city states

scavenger within a food web, scavengers are opportunist animals or birds that feed off dead animals e.g. vultures

scientific method an approach to experimentation in the sciences which relies on observation and testing hypotheses

Silk Road the ancient route that connected the Eurasian land mass via a network of roads

sustainability the processes that allow a system to be maintained into the future

transnational corporation (TNC) a large company operating internationally

trial by ordeal the process of putting someone on trial for an alleged crime by testing them with an ordeal that was often brutal

Acknowledgements

The Publishers would like to thank the following for permission to reproduce copyright material. Every effort has been made to trace all copyright holders, but if any have been inadvertently overlooked the Publishers will be pleased to make the necessary arrangements at the first opportunity.

Photo credits

p.2 *t* © Wavebreak Media Ltd/123RF; *b* © Wavebreak Media Ltd/123RF; **p.6** *t* © Iurii Kovalenko/123RF; *b* © Ira Berger/Alamy Stock Photo; **p.7** *t* © 36clicks/123RF; *b* © Dmitry Kalinovsky/123RF; **p.8** *l* © Age fotostock/Alamy Stock Photo; *r* © Bettmann/Getty Images; **p.10** *b* © HelloWorld Images Premium/Alamy Stock Photo; **p.11** © Lynn Johnson/National Geographic Creative/Alamy Stock Photo; **p.12** © Alexandr Blinov/123RF; **p.13** © ImageWorks/Topfoto; **p.14** © Kzenon/123RF; **p.16** © RIA Novosti/TopFoto; **p.17** *t* © Statista; *b* 01_12 © AFP; **p.18** © dpa picture alliance/Alamy Stock Photo; **p.20** *t* © Science & Society Picture Library/Getty Images; *b* © epa european pressphoto agency b.v./Alamy Stock Photo; **p.22** *l* © Albert Ziganshin/Shutterstock; *r* © egg design/Shutterstock; **p.24** © Aaron Huey/National Geographic/Getty Images; **p.25** © Carles Palle/Fotolia; **p.26** © Tom Thai/Moment Open/Getty Images; **p.28** *t* © Steven Prorak/123RF; *b* © Iakov Kalinin/123RF; **p.29** *t* © Patrick Lienin/123RF; *b* © teodoro ortiz tarrascusa/123RF; **p.30** © Robert Sulley; **p.31** *t* © Paul Aniszewski/123RF; *b* © 35007/E+/Getty Images; **p.32** © Galen Rowell/Mountain Light/Alamy Stock Photo; **p.33** © Dennis Hardley/Alamy Stock Photo; **p.34** © KIKE CALVO/TopFoto; **p.35** © Jane Sweeney/AWL Images/Getty Images; **p.39** *tr* © Dr Ken Macdonald/Science Photo Library; *tl* © Michael Ireland/Fotolia; *br* © rik58/Fotolia; *br* © Unclesam/Fotolia; **p.43** © WorldFoto/Alamy Stock Photo; **p.44** *t* © Angelo Gandolfi/naturepl.com/Nature Picture Library/Alamy Stock Photo; **p.45** © Yann Arthus-Bertrand/Getty Images; **p.46** © Sergei Uriadnikov/123RF; **p.47** *t* © epa european pressphoto agency b.v./Alamy Stock Photo; *b* © 2000 Topham Picturepoint/TopFoto; **p.48** © rawpixel/123RF; **p.49** © CartoonStock.com; **p.55** © Niday Picture Library/Alamy Stock Photo; **p.59** *l* © Photoservice Electa/Universal Images Group/REX/Shutterstock; *r* © TopFoto.co.uk; **p.62** © The Granger Collection/TopFoto; **p.64** *l* © World History Archive/Alamy Stock Photo; *r* © jorisvo/Fotolia; **p.66** © Stan Pritchard/Alamy Stock Photo; **p.68** *t* © DEA PICTURE LIBRARY/De Agostini/Getty Images; *b* © 2004 Credit:Fotomas/TopFoto; **p.70** *l* © Leemage/Universal Images Group/Getty Images; *tr* © philipus/Alamy Stock Photo; *br* © roberto fumagalli/MARKA/Alamy Stock Photo; **p.72** © Ted Wood/Aurora Photos/Alamy Stock Photo; **p.75** © Felis Images/Novarc Images/Alamy Stock Photo; **p.76** *l* © Angus Cepka; *r* © Print Collector/Hulton Archive/Getty Images; **p.78** © Igor Zakharevich/123RF; **p.80** © Taras Kushnir/123RF; **p.81** © maridav/123RF; **p.82** *bl* © hxdyl/123RF; *tr* © Photo Researchers, Inc/Alamy Stock Photo; **p.83** © 1xpert/123RF; **p.84** © Stapleton Historical Collection/HIP/TopFoto; **p.85** © Fine Art Images/HIP/TopFoto; **p.87** © Michael Rosskothen/123RF; **p.88** *l* © Fine Art Images/HIP/TopFoto; *tr* © DeAgostini/Getty Images; *br* © Dennis Cox/Alamy Stock Photo; **p.89** *tl* © ullsteinbild/TopFoto; *bl* © The Art Archive/Alamy Stock Photo; *r* © GL Archive/Alamy Stock Photo; **p.94** *l* © Florilegius/Alamy Stock Photo; **p.99** © Chronicle/Alamy Stock Photo; **p.100** *l* © United Archives/Topfoto; *r* © Library of Congress Prints and Photographs Division Washington; **p.101** © Roger-Viollet/Topfoto; **p.102** *l* © 2000 Credit:Topham Picturepoint/Topfoto; *tr* © Flight Collection/TopFoto; *br* © ITAR-TASS/TopFoto; **p.103** *t* © The Granger Collection/TopFoto; *b* © Peter Zheutlin; **p.104** © Predrag Vuckovic/Getty Images; **p.105** © StockTrek/Photodisc/Getty Images/Science; **p.108** © contrastwerkstatt/

Fotolia; **p.109** *l* © bapaume83/Fotolia; *r* © Getty Images/Image Source; **p.112** © Lou Linwei/Alamy Stock Photo; **p.114** © Ian Bracegirdle/iStockphoto; **p.117** © Matyas Rehak/123RF; **p.118** *t* © manfredxy/Fotolia; *b* © crackerclips/123RF; **p.121** *l* © Cahir Davitt/AWL Images/Getty Images; *r* © Matilde Gattoni/arabianEye FZ LLC/Alamy Stock Photo; **p.123** © Nicolas BERTHY/Fotolia; **p.124** © joe heller; **p.128** *l* © Suradin (Pinkblue) Suradingura/123RF; **p.129** *l* © Ponsulak Kunsub/123RF; *r* © potowizard/123RF; **p.130** *t* © PRISMA ARCHIVO/Alamy Stock Photo; *b* © Xinhua/Photoshot; **p.133** *l* © 916 collection/Alamy Stock Photo; *r* © Fine Art Images/Heritage Images/TopFoto; **p.134** *t* © British Library Board/TopFoto; *b* © The Print Collector/Alamy Stock Photo; **p.135** *l* © Fine Art Images/Heritage Images/TopFoto; *r* © Bill Ross/Corbis; **p.136** © Georgios Kollidas/123RF; **p.137** © Photodisc/Getty Images/World Commerce & Travel 5; **p.138** © Dennis Cox/Alamy Stock Photo; **p.139** © Matt Rourke/AP Photo/PA Images; **p.140** © Photo Researchers, Inc/Alamy Stock Photo; **p.143** © TPX/Prisma/Superstock; **p.144** © Wellcome Images/Wellcome Library, London; **p.145** © Frances Roberts/Alamy Stock Photo; **p.147** © Bibliothèque nationale de France

t = top, *b* = bottom, *l* = left, *r* = right, *c* = centre

Text credits

p.5 *Source A* data for internet usage map from We Are Social http://wearesocial.sg; **p.9** new words by permission. From Merriam-Webster's Collegiate® Dictionary, 11th Edition © 2016 by Merriam-Webster, Inc. (www.Merriam-Webster.com); **p.10** *Source A* data for map showing languages spoken around the world copyright mapsofworld.com; *Source C* www.unesco.org/new/fileadmin/MULTIMEDIA/HQ/CLT/pdf/FlyerEndangeredLanguages-WebVersion.pdf; **p.11** *Source D* Vice Media extract; *Source E* 'Globalization Helps Preserve Endangered Languages' by Mark Turin; December 2013 YaleGlobal Online; **p.18** *Source C* Whitaker Peace & Development Initiative; **p.21** *Source B* thediplomat.com; *Source C* psychologytoday.com; **p.43** *Source A* 'Change on the Pampas: Industrialized Farming Comes to Argentina' by Nicholas Kusnetz, North American Congress on Latin America (NACLA), 2009. Web; **p.50** *Source C* 'I was born into a world' by James Franco; **p.72** *Source B* history.com; **p.73** *Source D* extracts from 'The Secret History of the Mongols' by permission Cheng & Tsui Company; **p.74** *Source D* Changchun, translated by Arthur Waley; **p.94** *Source A* 'Sierra de la Plata: The Inca Legend of the Silver Mountain', 17 April 2015 www.ancient-origins.net/myths-legends-americas/sierra-de-la-plata-inca-legend-silver-mountain-002916; *Source D* extract from *History Today* reproduced by permission from the publisher; **p.98** *Source B* Hilke Fischer, '130 years ago: carving up Africa in Berlin' © DEUTSCHE WELLE. Used with permission; **p.114** *Source A* 'The Hidden Costs of Fossil Fuels' © Union of Concerned Scientists; **p.115** data for graph showing world energy production: OECD/IEA, Electricity Information 2014, IEA Publishing; **p.124** *Source A* www.greenpeace.org.uk/climate/wind-power; *Source C* 'Environmental Impacts of Wind Power' © Union of Concerned Scientists; *Source D* 'Wind Energy: Advantages and Disadvantages', 11 December 2014, Stanford University, Fall 2014, reproduced with permission from Dallas Lloyd; **p.125** *Source F* 'Eco-Blowback: Mutiny in the Land of Wind Turbines' by Matthias Schulz © 2016 Der Spiegel; **p.129** extract from 'Time: 100 Ideas That Changed the World' published by Time Inc.; **p.131** 'The revolutionary invention of the wheel', Ancient Origins, 2 June 2014 www.ancient-origins.net/ancient-technology/revolutionary-invention-wheel-001713; **p.138** extract from *How Did the Printing Press Change History?* published in Junior Scholastic, 30 March 2009. Copyright © 2009 by Scholastic Inc. Reproduced by permission. **p. 143** *Source A* extract from 'Time: 100 Ideas That Changed the World' published by Time Inc.; *Source B* 'Harrison's Clock – The Answer At Last' © The Open University; **p.144** *Source A* 'Edward Jenner' from Historyofvaccines.org, The College of Physicians of Philadelphia; **p.145** *Source C* extract about opposition to vaccination courtesy of Dr. Jenner's House, Museum and Garden

Visible Thinking – ideas, framework, protocol and thinking routines – from Project Zero at the Harvard Graduate School of Education have been used in many of our activities. You can find out more here: www.visiblethinkingpz.org.

Index

altitude 32
apex predators 38
architecture 76, 120, 133, 134, 135
arts 69, 76, 132, 133–5, 137

Bacon, Francis 140
Baghdad 69–70
Bayeux Tapestry 64
Beowulf 56, 68
Berlin Conference 98–9
biomes 26–33, 42–7
    climate, effect of 30–3
    location of 27
    types of 26, 28–9
Bird, Isabella 102
Black Death 67, 68
Bly, Nellie 103
Book of Knowledge of Ingenious Mechanical Devices 69, 70
Byzantine empire 58

Canterbury Tales (Chaucer) 57, 68
Catholic Church 65, 93
Charlemagne, Holy Roman Emperor 59
Chaucer, Geoffrey 57, 68
China 75–6, 85
Christianity 58, 59
classicism 133
climate: biomes, effect on 30–3
climate change 46, 49, 114

climate graphs 34–5, 37
Clovis, King of Franks 59
cold deserts 28
colonialism 47, 98
Columbian Exchange 92, 93, 95
Columbus, Christopher 88, 90
communications 6, 96
conflict 46
Confucius 75
Congo Basin, Africa 45–6
conquistadors 93–4
Constantine, Byzantine emperor 58
consumers (ecosystems) 38
continuity 57
Copernicus, Nicolaus 138
Crusades 70

da Gama, Vasco 89, 90
Da Vinci, Leonardo 135, 136
Dark Ages 58
decomposers (ecosystems) 38
deforestation 46
Democratic Republic of Congo (DRC) 45, 46, 47
Dene, William 68
desert biomes 27, 28
Dias, Bartolemeu 88, 90
Domesday Book 66
Drake, Francis 89, 90

Earhart, Amelia 102
economic resources 112
ecosystems 38
electricity 110, 113, 115, 116–19, 122, 124–5, 140, 142
empiricism 140
encyclopedias 142
Enlightenment 140–7
environments 24–51
    biomes 26–33, 42–7
    climate change and 49
    climate graphs 34–5, 37
    ecosystems 38
    food webs 38, 40–1
    human impact on 42–3
    and sustainability 51
exploration 80–105
    Age of Exploration 84, 87–90
    Columbian Exchange 92–5
    conquistadors 93–4
    effect on early societies 84–6
    imperial expansion 98–9
    industrialization and 96–7
    key figures 88–9, 102–3
    reasons for 82–3
    space exploration 104–5
    tourism 100–1
    21st-century exploration 104

feudal system 60–2
food webs 38, 40–1
forests 27, 29, 45–6
franchises 12
Franco, James 50
Froissart, Jean 62

Galileo Galilei   138–9, 140
gaming industry   20–1
gauchos   42, 44
Genghis Khan   71–4
Geoffrey le Baker   68
geothermal power   116, 122–3
globalization   2–23
    causes of   6–7
    definition of   4
    effect on gaming industry   20–1
    effect on language   9–11
    effect on sport   16–18
    in history   8
    transnational corporations   12–13, 16
globetrotting   100–1
grassland biomes   27, 28, 42–4
gravity   142, 143
Gutenberg, Johannes   138

Harrison, John   142, 143
Hastings, Battle of   64
Historia Roffensis (William Dene)   68
Hobbes, Thomas   146
hot deserts   28
House of Wisdom, Baghdad   69, 70
humanism   133
human resources   112
hydroelectric power (HEP)   116–17

ideas (innovations)   129–48
    definition of   130–1
    Enlightenment   140–7
    Renaissance   132–9
infographics   19
innovations, *see* ideas (innovations)

internet   4, 5, 6, 11, 20–1
invasions: medieval   64
Islam   69–70
Itaipu Dam   117
Italy   132–3, 135–7

Jenner, Edward   142, 144
Joan of Arc   55
Justinian, Byzantine emperor   58, 59

Kingdom of Franks   59
Kipling, Rudyard   100

labour availability   7
language: globalization and   9–11
latitude   30, 143
legal system: medieval   65
Ljubljana Marshes Wheel   130, 131
Locke, John   146
Londonderry, Annie   103
longitude   142, 143

Machiavelli, Nicholas   137
Magellan, Ferdinand   89, 90
marine biomes   26
maritime effect   32
maritime exploration   87–90
Masdar City, Abu Dhabi   120–1
Masefield, John   82
Michelangelo   137
Middle Ages   55–76
    China, life in   75–6
    dates   56–7
    empires, expansion of   69–74
    life during   64–8
    Roman empire, decline of   58–9
    society, structure of   60–2

Middle Kingdom, China   75–6
migration   7
mining   46
Mongol empire   71–4

natural resources   110–11: *see also* renewable energy
natural world   135
Newton, Isaac   142, 143
non-renewable energy   110, 113–15
non-renewable resources   110
nuclear power   113

ocean currents   33
Ottoman empire   58, 87, 98, 132

Pampas region, South America   42–4
Pax Mongolica   71
perspective (art)   134
Petrarch, Francesco   133
pilgrimages   65
polar deserts   28
politics
    and Enlightenment   146–7
    political instability   46
pollution   113–14
Polo, Marco   85–6, 138
printing press   138
producers (ecosystems)   38

rainforest biomes   27, 29, 45–6
religion   58, 59, 65, 69–70, 93
Renaissance   87, 132–9
renewable energy   110, 116–25
renewable resources   110

resources   46, 110–13
road building   46
Roman empire: decline of   56, 58–9
Rousseau, Jean-Jacques   146, 147

savannahs (tropical grasslands)   27, 28
scavengers (ecosystems)   38
science: developments in   140–5
scientific method   140–1, 142
Scientific Revolution   138
Silk Road   67, 84
solar power   116, 118
Song Dynasty, China   75, 76
space exploration   104–5
sport: and globalization   16–18

sustainability   108–25
　environments and   51
　natural resources   110–11
　non-renewable energy   113–15
　renewable energy   116–25
sustainable resources   110

taiga forests 27
temperate forests   27
temperate grasslands   28
Tereshkova, Valentina   102
tourism   100–1
trade   7, 65, 69, 71, 72, 82, 84, 87
transnational corporations (TNCs)   12–13, 16
transport   6, 8, 65, 96–7, 100

tropical grasslands (savannahs)   27, 28
tundra   27, 29

vaccination   142, 144–5
Verne, Jules   100, 101

wheel, invention of   130–1
Whitaker, Forest   18
William the Conqueror (William I)   64, 66
wind power   116, 119, 124–5
women, role of   65, 71, 76
World Trade Organization (WTO)   7

Zheng He   88